# MASTER YOUR PATIENCE:

## A PRACTICAL GUIDE TO MANAGE YOUR SKILLS

*To our family,*

*our friends,*

*our colleagues.*

*Our main sources of inspiration.*

# Dr. Pedro COSTA

## Specialized physician

Otorhinolaryngology and cervicofacial surgery, Belgium

Mindfulness-based cognitive therapy (MBCT)

*Author*

## Graça COSTA

### Master and Doctor in Anthropology

Architect, Federal University of Pernambuco, Recife, Brazil

Fine artist

Drawing and graphic design teacher, Federal Institute of Technological Education-IFPE, Recife, PE, Brazil

# | PREFACE |

## Nun Coen

Patience is one of the six paramitas, or six perfections, in the teachings of Buddha.

Buddha attained enlightenment and lived in India over 2,600 years ago.

He taught that there are six perfections that take us from the edge of suffering to the edge of tranquility.

One of these perfections is patience—or *kshanti* in Sanskrit.

Full patience does not mean enduring the unendurable, resigning, or remaining quiet while waiting for changes.

On the contrary, it is the ability to recognize what is happening with yourself, with everyone else, and with the world and to welcome and transform it.

As the Brazilian educator Paulo Freire taught, hope must be active and not passive.

What can we do to turn impatience into patience?

Patience is to wait, appease, create causes and conditions for change to occur in an adequate, smooth way without insults, hatred, impatience, aversions, exclusions, or cancellations.

In this book, Pedro Costa makes an important analysis—an anamnesis of altered states of consciousness and offers guidelines and suggestions so that we can perceive our moods and develop the ability to cope with them.

Patience is essential to have physical, mental, and social health.

If we break the word apart, we find the science of peace.

Inner and outer peace.

Creating conditions for more harmonious, lasting, and sincere relationships.

Being aware of peace is the result of proper training.

We need to know ourselves in depth and understand the intricacies of the mind and know how to deal with altered states.

The natural state of mind is without attachments and aversions, without haste, despair, or anxiety.

Like a ground zero.

From stimuli—both internal and external—we leave the neutral point of ground zero, and we can move forward or backward.

When changing gears in an automobile, we need to listen to the engine, wait for the right moment to change gears or direction.

It requires training in patience, in a certain amount of waiting, in mindfulness.

Pure presence is key for me.

To be absolutely present in the current moment.

Without haste, but with urgency, observing, investigating, understanding, and acting.

Not just reacting to the provocations of the world, but making decisions on how to respond to those provocations.

The six perfections, teachings left by Buddha, are mutually complementary, and one does not exist without the other.

*Dana*—donation, generosity, offering; *shila*—precepts, ethical life; *kshanti*—patience; *virya*—right effort, perseverance; *dhyana*—meditation; *prajna*—understanding.

When we manage to unite and use all these perfect virtues, we will be absolutely in the present and each of the perfections will be realized.

With great joy, I received an invitation from Pedro Costa to say a few words about this work.

I am a Zen Buddhist nun and I do not work directly with mindfulness.

In fact, my tradition strongly stresses the understanding of the void and realizing mind emptiness—where everything flows with nothing fixed or permanent.

Full attention, called *darana* in yoga, is a prerequisite for the meditative practices called zen.

Sitting down in zen state—the practice of *zazen*—means getting in touch with yourself.

It includes mindfulness and the ability to change your state of mind through knowledge, understanding, compassion, and wisdom.

Buddha also left us teachings on how to develop patience: *maitri* (love), *karuna* (compassion), *mudita* (joy), and *upeksha* (equanimity).

Developing these thoughts and qualities entails expanding consciousness and allowing the manifestation of unlimited compassion: to know how to welcome, acknowledge, accept, and transform. This prevents suffering and pain.

Patience is the greatest gift we can offer the world and all the people with whom we interact directly or indirectly.

Shall we train it?

Open this book, read, try, repeat, learn, and develop your ability to transform reality through love, compassion, joy of living, and equanimity—recognizing that all beings, all forms of life, have the same right to live and manifest.

Remember also that nothing is permanent and everything is intertwined.

We are Earth's life and with all beings we can learn to wait for the right time and create causes and conditions for growth.

When a person changes, all of humanity takes a step towards that transformation.

We are capable of so much. We can change reality.

Awaken. Arise.

Follow the instructions and develop mindfulness.

It is pure presence training.

I stress: read, understand, and follow the recommendations.

There are no harmful side effects.

Quite the contrary.

All secondary effects will be beneficial and will lead us to a culture of peace, justice, and healing for the Earth and all beings.

Practice is not separate from realization.

Hands in prayer,

**Nun Coen**

# | INTRODUCTION |

# | INTRODUCTION |

We experience, still in our mothers' womb, moments of waiting: swimming in fertile liquid, listening to sounds we do not understand, acquiring shape and knowledge, growing and developing. For many months, even without any notion of it, nature gives us its first lessons about the importance of allying ourselves with time, so necessary for maturation, until we are able to cross the limits of the reality of birth. From then on, we continually face feelings, actions, and situations that require us to make a constant effort to develop an essential quality to face the most diverse circumstances of life: patience.

From a very early age, this word serves as an instrument to shape our personality, our actions, and our reactions—"Have patience, son"; "be patient!"; "patience!" In turn, we are molded into a being that adapts to the most diverse situations. In a constant struggle between the *I* and the *other*, which requires adaptation and control in the face of difficult moments, we work daily to develop tolerance to the obstacles that arise in our daily lives.

Patience is a virtue, a gift, a feeling, but it is also a construction, a learning, an individual exercise that directly interferes in our life, in our social relationships, and in our happiness.

Patience is the secret ingredient that enriches life. Easygoing and tolerant, patience is a dedicated friend who gives us time to appreciate our experiences and deepen our involvement in everything we do. In turn, impatience has a hard and heavy nature that weakens the body and mind.

When we impatiently pursue a goal, our breathing becomes rapid and abrupt, our movements become hasty, and our thoughts become somewhat out of control. When we are impatient, we look like spoiled brats who think they will always get what they want, when they want it. In an immature way, when faced with obstacles or problems that cannot be overcome immediately we are surprised and feel defeated.

The term "full patience" has a perfect meaning. There is no such thing as being partially "calm." If the way to manage patience is not complete, we will lose it, and thus show our impatience. If you want to tame your patience, do it completely. Together, we will build this path of questioning and understanding. This reading will bring a better understanding of full patience and its relationship with the practice of mindfulness.

Since we believe in this constructive process, we decided to try to dialogue with our own feelings and experiences as parents, children, friends, and professionals—in short, beings who seek ways of learning and realization—to bring our concerns and thoughts to the reader. We do not seek to create a formula, but rather we seek to stimulate thoughts that lead us to a better understanding of the ways that can lead us to improve our patience.

First, learn to recognize the way impatience arises. The people around you and the lack of time are the most valuable teachers when it comes to training patience. Try to listen carefully to your anxiety, as this can be a useful sign, indicating that you need to relax and let go of the expectations you have about yourself or about others and about the time that runs through your life. Keep in mind that through patience, difficulties can be used to your advantage.

## But what is patience after all?

A practical definition of patience is that it is the ability to tolerate or accept a difficulty, delay, or worry without becoming frustrated or without changing one's mood. Generally, no person escapes any of these situations: delays, worries, frustrations, or mood swings. Such situations are a part of life, whether we like it or not.

To better understand the realm of patience, we introduce the notion of "enemies of patience" and "friends of patience."

One's "enemies of patience" can be, and must be, identified. They are defined as the main "culprits" of our daily unrest: first, the people; second, time; and third, situations. The fourth culprit is a combination of the first three: chaos, or "people short of time in difficult situations." Usually, when we completely run out of patience, we reach this last stage of impatience, and this set of factors distresses us.

We realize that this reaction of losing patience only makes an already stressful and unpleasant situation worse. We then begin to make a conscious effort to respond differently to delays, difficulties, or concerns. Often, the best we can do is simply tolerate the presence of the "enemies of patience." To do so, we have to understand them better.

Finally, as we continue to exercise and practice mindfulness, by focusing on the elements of the present, we are able to accept them as part of life. To this end, we need to broaden our perception of the world and our behavior in the face of difficulties, allying ourselves with what we call "friends of patience."

We describe a simple method—the "4S" rule—to ensure you never forget these "good companions." The four "friends of patience" are silence, sigh, smile, and sure. Easy, right? We detail this method and each of the four friends, in addition to the enemies, in the following chapters. We also observe that the more we focus on the present, living the here and now, the more likely we are to find the "friends of patience."

## Why full patience?

We have been studying the guidelines given by scholars and practitioners on the importance of implementing mindfulness in our lives based on techniques that lead us to live in the present, valuing each moment intensely. Mindfulness proposes that we exercise daily, routine habits to stay focused on what we are doing, without letting our mind wander into past memories or future accomplishments. Our senses must be connected to the *here* and *now*, to the environment and people around us, to the actions we are performing, and to our body and mind without distractions.

The constant application of mindfulness techniques reveals physical and emotional benefits, even for those who do not effectively practice yoga or meditation. Although these guidelines were originally found in eastern religions, particularly Buddhism, any individual who is determined to fully experience the present, regardless of their religious beliefs, can reap the benefits that will help them lead a happier existence.

We started to practice and study more about these guidelines, and we concluded that living in mindfulness is important. By expanding our knowledge and considering the entire universe, we realized the importance of observing the real value of being "here and now," but doing so patiently. What is the point of focusing our attention on the present, focusing meticulously on the activities we carry out, connecting carefully with our daily lives, observing the environment that surrounds us with caution, if we are doing it full of irritation, anguish, and discontent? We reiterate that to exercise patience it is necessary to focus on the moment one is experiencing and, based on reflection and daily exercise, tread paths that lead to increased resilience, benevolence, forgiveness, and compassion, which are the foundations of patience. Thus, mindfulness makes itself present in patience.

In this book, we highlight the value of full patience and share this learning process with you.

## Thinking a little more about the importance of patience...

We emphasize that resilience, benevolence, forgiveness, and compassion are the foundations of patience. While these are important precepts in various religions, we do not intend to detail religious norms and conduct. We believe that whatever the reader's religious beliefs, or lack thereof, we are able to demonstrate the importance of being happy with the experience of these foundations in our lives. The examples we use to illustrate the ideas about full patience reveal, even in a subliminal way, instruments for self-knowledge and happiness, which are important goals for human beings. We slightly emphasize some of these precepts, as in the following text about compassion. Being patient is a way of experiencing compassion. Compassion is an act that reaches out to those who suffer, including ourselves. We suffer when we are impatient, because our lack of patience creates unnecessary stress in our life. Therefore, cultivating patience is a way of taking care of yourself—in other words, it is a form of self-compassion. Understanding impatience and managing our attitudes to bring about calm will lead us to a more peaceful life with ourselves and with others, both today and in the future. To reiterate, more patience means less unnecessary daily frustration and a happier life.

We know that reading a book to the end requires a significant amount of patience, time, and attention.

One cannot merely skip or skim the content, as we do with our messages and texts on cell phones. Instead, we invite you to read this book to the end and in its entirety, with full awareness.

# | MEDICINE AND PATIENCE |

Any of us can be doctors, even without the formal title. For example, we serve as care-givers by taking care of ourselves and others. Medicine, in the academic and professional scope, requires a significant amount of dedication. The most important is not the amount of knowledge acquired, but the quality of the trained professional, which requires constant care in our attitudes towards others, our friends, and family as well as towards our patients and professional colleagues. A good doctor should improve the way they interact with their patients, and patience is a great ally in this process.

Training with a guided program in mindfulness-based cognitive therapy (MBCT) allowed me to become familiar with this rich area and to better understand the value of patience. We believe that the practice of mindfulness meditation and medicine mainly applied to the improvement of patience are tools of wisdom that are cultivated and strengthened both for our growth and for the good of others. Both require in-depth scientific knowledge and real learning in daily practice. In a daily life full of banal relationships and stressful coexistence, having patience means standing out among a majority that does not realize its real value. Our quality of life and our mental health will only significantly improve if we pay attention to our reactions to our environment and apply the know-how to our interactions with the people around us.

The way people treat each other has changed over the decades. Things have become faster, instant, colder, and less personal. Selfishness and intolerance have both increased. Consequently, we have become more impatient, as we get used to having communication and information immediately. All these changes have resulted in affecting and weakening human relationships, increasing the amount of unnecessary arguments, and making attrition more frequent.

In many books, the quality of a "good doctor" is related to the ability to be a cultured, patient, and prudent professional. Science is a necessary asset for medical practice, and it is indispensable for reaching its goal in search of the truth. Furthermore, to be a good doctor it is also essential to understand and cultivate patience. We usually speak of the sick as "patients," and the virtue of patience is mandatory regarding health and the contact with the world of caregivers. Illness is often described as a "school for patience," which forces us to have a new attitude towards life. From this viewpoint, the art of caregiving entails eliminating impatience, a sign of maladies caused by an immaturity that has not yet been overcome.

Caregivers, like doctors or other health professionals, must be patient in the same way as those under their care. Patience is an instrument of healing, both for doctors and for those who seek to improve and maintain their health and happiness.

# | ANTHROPOLOGY AND PATIENCE |

Anthropology is a science that studies human beings both in relation to their physical nature, origins, and evolution as well as to the relationships they develop as social beings and makers of culture.

Dialoguing with different areas of science, anthropology develops close interdisciplinary relations with sociology, history, law, economics, psychology, geography, biology, linguistics, medicine, astronomy, and the arts in general, among other fields of study and research. Anthropologists collaborate with professionals from these fields as they pursue diverse activities.

In this anthropological universe, how are humans related to the theme of the current work? How are links weaved between the human being and patience, from the point of view of anthropology? This answer is found in the different fields of anthropological study.

In **religion** and different belief systems, faith has patience as an ally to face and overcome adversity and to understand nature and the supernatural, the material and the spiritual, and life and death.

In systems of **kinship**, family relationships, and the processes of marriage and descent, a complex web of actions and reactions involve patience.

In studies on **linguistics**, the body that speaks and expresses patience, or the lack of it, generates a system of signs to communicate.

In investigations about **popular culture**, the preparation of festivities, the elaboration of costumes, the silence of the masked people, and the participation in cultural events and contests involve the remarkable presence of patience as an indispensable element.

Studies on **gender** and its wide universe of relationships entail a complex discussion about diversity, acceptance, and tolerance. This triad of elements is also based on patience and respect.

These few examples are a small sample of the grandeur of the discussions that can be raised by the intersection of anthropology and patience.

Although our objective is not to make an in-depth study about humans and patience, we build a simple outline on the importance of this theme and primarily focus on helping individuals achieve a more pleasant and meditative daily life.

# | IMPATIENCE |

# | IMPATIENCE |

> "All human errors are impatience,
> a premature breaking off
> of methodical procedure."
>
> *Franz Kafka*

## What is impatience?

Impatience is nothing more than a lack of patience. It is related to an "inability to suffer," to a state of permanent worry that prevents peace and relaxation, to a constant annoyance that borders on irritability, or to the hustle to reach a certain goal, whatever the cost.

## How can impatience harm us?

The harmful aspects of impatience can hurt us significantly, especially when it takes us away from our goals. Being impatient can even cause problems to our health; obesity, hypertension, and premature aging are among the ills associated with a lack of calm. Impatience and obesity are directly linked. Easy access to unhealthy (and generally quite tasty) food is often used by people with a "short temper" as a way to deal with stress.

Being impatient with certain types of situations is natural. However, when impatience occurs frequently, it is important to understand its causes to treat the issue objectively, with inquiry and through personal changes. Being a more patient person, in addition to benefiting those with whom we live, also allows us to live more peacefully and happily.

First, we address some aspects of daily life that trigger impatience.

**What does it feel like when we realize that reaching a certain goal will cost more than we originally thought?**

For many people, the act of doing nothing and being idle can bring impatience, but first, we explore another context.

Imagine you are sitting in your living room with an empty mind, for example, just allowing yourself to relax and be present, with nothing to do or fear, with no immediate plans or expectations.

Now, imagine that you decide to go out and do something fun. At this point, you have adopted a goal. You are not yet impatient, but you may be starting this process.

Suppose you call a friend to see if they are available to hang out with you. This generates expectation and a certain anxiety. The longer it takes to find someone to hang out with, the more restless you become.

Another simple but commonplace example is when a child is waiting for Christmas, and they cannot think of other things. Through this anxiety, they generate a disquiet that is not healthy. Waiting for Christmas is costing them more than they thought, in terms of their ability to pay attention to other things in the meantime. It is an unconscious attitude, but it generates impatience.

Another example is that you start writing a book and think it will take you approximately six months to finish. You are on schedule, but you have an idea for an even better book. Then you realize that continuing to write the first book is interfering with the opportunity to work on the second book, and imagining that second book is also interfering with the ongoing book. You start to become impatient.

In another situation, you are driving home and think it will only take you 20 minutes. However, the two cars in front of you are going only 10 miles an hour, well below the speed limit. To make matters worse, they are driving side by side in the only two lanes available. You realize it will take you longer than you thought to get home, which triggers your impatience.

Furthermore, impatience and outrage are a dangerous combination. Imagine that you are at a supermarket checkout. You choose a queue and find that it does not move, compared to the others next to it. You start to get impatient and observe the reasons for the delay. Then you notice that the cashier in your queue is chatting with a coworker. In addition to being impatient, you start to become outraged and decide to move to another queue, blaming the employee for your delay.

Surely, if you had been warned about a problem with the cash register in the queue you had chosen, you would have changed queues with less irritation. In that situation, you considered the employee and her side conversation to be responsible for your delay and your impatience. The issue was not only lost time, but it was compounded by what caused the delay to reach the cashier.

### Major Signs of Impatience

On a scale of 0 to 10, how patient do you consider yourself? Consider the following main signs of impatience, and if you tend to feel this way often. Beware of **ALIOTH**.

**A**lways hurrying

**L**egs and feet shaking

**I**rritability

**O**utbursts

**T**ense muscles

**H**ard breathing

An infinite number of small situations could affect us on a daily basis, making us cross the threshold between calm and impatience.

Impatience motivates us to reduce our efforts to reach or change our goals.

When we experience impatience, we start to activate different strategies to reduce our anxiety, and sometimes, we create ineffective ways to minimize the problems we face.

Some of the examples highlight that having more than one path to solve a problem generates anxiety and impatience. Stand in line or switch cashiers? Continue writing the first book and complete it, or stop and start writing another one? Continue driving behind a slow car or change lanes at the first opportunity? The existence of several possibilities for solutions causes us to be affected by impatience and anxiety.

Therefore, we must be aware of how we cope with the problems that worry us and how we generate new strategies to solve them. In doing so, caution and awareness should be exercised continuously.

**Treat impatience as a warning.**

Impatience has a certain type of benefit as it serves as an alarm, and it is in our behavioral repertoire for a reason. Sometimes we are working on a project that is going nowhere, and we need to accept it and change our focus. Sometimes we are behind a slow car and the other lane is free, so we could change lanes or take another route. In another moment we feel impatient because we are in a relationship with no way out, and we need to hasten to find a solution so that both parties can be happier. The examples are numerous.

**How to deal with impatience? Self-knowledge gives us power.**

Once we understand how impatience works, we give ourselves the chance to manage it better. We need to put our "impatient energy" to use at the right time: when we need to speed things up or change our course. However, we need to learn to calm our lack of patience and to become self-aware to cope with the limitations that we meet.

Knowledge is a gift, an instrument, a weapon. Knowing how impatience works allows us to better find balance so that we can follow our paths in peace and with confidence.

In a fast-paced world and in a society that values speed, it is possible to feel uncomfortable with slowness. Patience is a skill like any other, which must be learned, and it entails accepting the events of life that we cannot change.

Whether at work or elsewhere, stressful situations abound and seem to leave no room for things to unfold at their own pace: we must always do everything faster and with less time, less money, and less support from our colleagues or relatives. How does that affect us? The consequences of impatience are endless. However, to benefit from this behavior, it is necessary to understand our responses to difficult situations and the people around us as these affect us considerably. Conquering patience requires knowing our impatience threshold.

**By better understanding impatience we are able to broaden the definitions of patience.**

Patience is seeing life as something different, not as an endless series of problems that must be solved quickly. The solution is to understand that change is not an event, but a process. We should not, for example, begin the experience of learning new wellness practices, such as mindfulness meditation, by expecting quick changes or immediate and lasting benefits. Solving longstanding problems in a few meditation sessions is difficult. Thus, the conscious practice of patience requires knowing how to swim in the waters of impatience without drowning and how to change by using mindfulness and by allying with the friends of patience. With the "4S" method, the friends of patience, we offer ourselves tools to dismantle the gears of impatience.

To begin consciously practicing this method, one must learn to observe the effects of impatience on the body and mind by considering the following questions:

How does this act on my body?

How does it appear in my thoughts?

How does it affect my behavior towards others?

When we observe the bodily effects of impatience—which are manifested by muscular tensions, agitation, explosions (remember "ALIOTH")—it is our responsibility to control these conditionings to act in a different way.

Impatience is among the major risk factors for high blood pressure in young adults. We constantly feel that situations are urgent, and we suffer from anxiety and losing our cool. We end up acting in a turbulent and confused way in the face of these difficulties. Patience, our ally in this fight, is a skill to be developed in everyday life with simple exercises such as empathy and breath control.

Patience is a decision. It requires questioning the demands placed on ourselves and on others. In any situation, being patient is also knowing the difference between what we can control and what we cannot. For example, we have no control over the delay in traffic due to an accident, but we do have control over how we react in full awareness of the facts. Does this delay depend only on us? Could we have woken up earlier to avoid the traffic? In reality, we are solely accountable for our reactions to any situation. This is the essence of our "responsibility" or "responsiveness," and this characteristic makes us conscious beings.

If impatience is described as looking forward to the future, patience is considered attention focused on the present. Full patience is the combination of these factors that leads to a more balanced life. Why do we try to hurry to an uncontrollable future, circumventing the way we live now? Why not try to find ways that help us deal with impatience by practicing full patience? In mindfulness, patience is one of the seven pillars addressed. Between the stimulus and the response, you can make a conscious choice to breathe and calm down, which brings you to the present. We need to learn to perceive the birth of impatience in ourselves so that it gradually becomes easier to step out of our habitual conditioning and to allow ourselves to accept each moment in its fullness. By observing and identifying the four "enemies of patience" without judgment, we will have better control to choose our reactions when impatience manifests itself.

This book demonstrates that by separating these four elements you can identify who or what is causing your impatience. It is like a game of tug of war: the four friends against the four foes. One group pulls one way and the other pulls the opposite until the rope breaks or one group has more strength to pull the other into the mud.

Since the fourth enemy of patience is the sum of the other three opponents, the enemy's team has a certain "advantage" to win. It is therefore necessary that you actively fight back and know how to play this game.

| FRIENDS OF PATIENCE 4S | ENEMIES OF PATIENCE |
| --- | --- |
| SILENCE | PEOPLE |
| SIGH | TIME |
| SMILE | SITUATIONS |
| SURE | PEOPLE WITHOUT TIME IN DIFFICULT SITUA-TIONS (CHAOS) |

Practicing mindfulness allows us to experience increasing kindness to ourselves. Despite our emotions, limits, self-criticism, or weaknesses, we deserve to treat ourselves with kindness. This practice also promotes greater benevolence toward others. Patience reminds us that we have the ability to decide at any time how to respond to circumstances, that not all our demands are right, that we have to plan tasks better so that we are not overwhelmed, and that our impatience impacts those around us. Moreover, change is a path to mindfulness, not a predetermined destination.

**"Impatience teaches us that patience is the only solution."**

When a person allows themself to be overcome by impatience, they will never discover what was in store for their life. It is necessary to wait patiently, however difficult and distressing this action may seem.

**How does impatience and emotional intelligence help you?**

Understanding how to best deal with impatience requires developing a skill. When a person practices self-knowledge, they come to know who they really are, and they are able to better control their feelings and to understand the origin of such feelings and how to use them in the best way.

This ability is called emotional intelligence. People with this skill find it easy to get along with impatient individuals and to deal with their own lack of patience in a healthier and more assertive way. They do not get upset as easily, and they lose their cool less often when dealing with difficult people and situations. They learn self-control techniques (e.g., the "4S" technique), choosing their responses and attitudes better, because they know that there is a right way and time to achieve their goals.

Have you started to understand that finding the reason for your impatience is important? Impatience arises when a situation does not go the way we want or when people or our environment do not live up to our expectations. Our expectations are often disconnected from reality, and recognizing this aspect is the first step towards mindfulness.

To identify what caused your impatience, you must find the cause of your lack of patience among the three main reasons:

- **People**
- **Time**
- **Difficult situations**

Impatience greatly hinders our perception of our goals and our relationships. Haste exposes all our weaknesses. Do not let that feeling control your life and make decisions for you.

How about starting to think about changes?

We guide you on this journey of reflections, inquiry, and learning.

## Recognize when you are impatient.

It will not necessarily be easy at first. When certain things do not go the way we want—for example, when there is traffic, the elevator gets stuck, or an important correspondence takes a long time to arrive—we tend to think that the cause of our impatience is external to us. Start by noting that your impatience is merely an automatic response when you do not get what you want right away. An impulsive response from your mental aspect that remains "on auto-pilot."

You probably know most of the triggers that trigger your impatience. This could be having to wait for a date, getting stuck in a long line, having trouble solving a computer problem, or talking with someone about a topic that does not interest you. While the motives are external, impatience grows inside you.

# | THE FOUR FRIENDS OF PA-TIENCE |

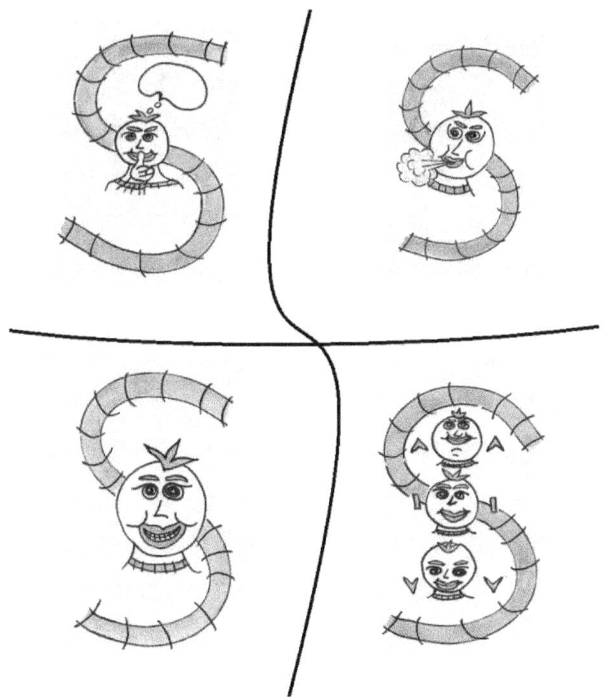

# - 1 -

# | THE FOUR FRIENDS OF PATIENCE: "4S" |

"Patience is the strength of the weak
and impatience the weakness of the strong."

*Immanuel Kant*

The four friends of patience are the basis of the "4S" method:

SILENCE
SIGH
SMILE
SURE

This method is a mnemonic—a set of techniques used to aid the memorization process. It consists of the elaboration of supports, such as schemes, graphics, symbols, words or phrases related to the subject that is intended to be memorized. Using these supports allows a quick association and a better assimilation of the content.

It has been proven that human memory stores information more easily when it is associated with organized and simple sequences, which help to effectively record data. Mnemonics are created freely, as long as they make sense to the person who memorizes them. However, the result will not be effective for complicated sequences.

**How does a mnemonic device work?**

In practice, mnemonic means intervening during the following three main stages of memorization:

- When information is transmitted during encoding, the brain transforms the raw data into something more meaningful through a pre-assimilation of information. This stage depends on one's attention and emotional state.

- During the time of storage, the brain sorts the information and archives it.

- Finally, at the time of retrieval, the brain empties the recorded information and restores it. The association performed previously plays a key role during this operation.

Mnemonic teaching has been shown to be an effective, evidence-based practice in improving learning and memorization. Next, we further explain the implications of the "4S" mnemonic in mindfulness.

## THE FOUR "FRIENDS OF PATIENCE"

The "4S" method is used to facilitate your response, both physical and mental, in a situation in which you are accustomed to react impatiently. In such situations, the four "friends of patience" will help you deal with the "enemies of patience."

A person's patient action in a given unwanted situation must be complete. Signs elicited through our words, gestures, expressions, and breathing all indicate that we have lost our patience. These four "friends of patience" are the key to demonstrating and cultivating full patience. The following chapters explain that each of these words is fundamentally important in our lives.

**The "4S" method is simple:**

**SILENCE**
**SIGH**
**SMILE**
**SURE**

The following scenario summarizes this method: imagine your husband or boyfriend comes home late, angry and tired. He's had a rough day, so he asks to be left alone for a while to take a hot shower while you fix him something to eat. You go to the kitchen, tired from your busy day at work. It was one of those Mondays, stressful and on the clock, with projects that did not go as you planned. After the meal, you head to your room to enjoy a restful night's sleep, since you only have five hours to sleep, because tomorrow you wake up early for work.

Arriving in the bedroom, you discover a wet towel placed on top of your side of the bed, forgotten by your husband. It is late, you are exhausted, and you are facing a situation you have experienced before. Your husband is in the living room watching his favorite TV show.

**What do you do in this situation?**

You go downstairs to show him the towel. You speak loudly as he is far away, in the other room. Your breathing is heavy and you wait for a fair explanation. Arriving in the room, you shake your head in a negative way, disapproving of his sloppy attitude, and with a frown you say that this is unacceptable. In this situation, the four "enemies of patience" are present. Someone (your husband) repeated a *difficult situation* at a moment when *time* was precious (for your sleep).

In a similar situation, anyone would easily become irritated. However, it is not worth reacting in this way because it is almost midnight, and you need rest and peace. There is a reason to be angry, but perhaps it is better to react in a different way.

This is where the "4S" method comes in. Here is the answer you could develop in a situation like this:

SILENCE—Say nothing.

SIGH—Take four deep breaths through your nose.

SMILE—When you meet him again, smile sincerely and without sarcasm.

SURE—Shake your head up and down at the moment of loss of patience: you accept that this is a real situation and that this can happen again. This acceptance serves to affirm your well-being and prioritize your peace.

You must be wondering if this kind of attitude is a form of weakness, a lack of strength. Would that be a case of fear of getting into conflicts? The answer is no. It is only one way to develop the desired full patience.

If you face many similar situations, if you feel that the limits of your patience are being tested, if you want to be more tolerant in your daily life, this is a method to help you stop being so impulsive. Furthermore, it is a process to make changes.

Before nervousness and its consequences arise, turn to the four friends of patience. They are there to help you.

The following chapters detail each of the four friends to help you understand how these partners work and to make it easier to memorize the "4S" method. Next, we analyze in more detail the four "enemies of patience," which include *people, time, situations*, and *chaos*, which is the combination of these three enemies.

# | SILENCE |

# | **SILENCE** |

"Silence is the element
in which great things
fashion themselves together."

*Maurice Maeterlinck*

We give ourselves and others a moment of silence. To ease the pressure, we become aware of our breath, our body, and allow ourselves a quiet time in our mind.

**How is this possible? Shall we exercise?**

In a quiet place, sit silently with yourself and ask yourself, "What is happening to me?" Thanks to our bodies' warnings, we know what state we are in: sad, angry, depressed, aggressive, or impatient. Becoming aware of our emotional state is far more beneficial than hiding it.

1. Close your eyes.

2. Inhale through your nose as you inflate your chest like a balloon.

3. Hold your breath for a second and then let the air out slowly through your mouth, as if blowing through a straw. Watch the feeling of impatience dissipate on the exhalation.

Take the time to take at least five deep breaths to lower your heart rate.

Brilliant orators are not just wizards of words, they are also a master of silence. Learning silence is fundamental yet so paradoxical. Learning to be silent is much more difficult than speaking. If children are afraid of the dark, adults are afraid of the lack of words: silence.

Here are some elements in favor of silence in speech: in silence, we remain in contact with the other, present even in a non-verbal state. This extends to the importance of working on your physical presence by incorporating the following steps of the "friends of patience": breathing, smiling, and nodding yes, with an affirmative gesture of the head. Silence should be the first friend to be remembered. Silence is a moment you give yourself to anchor, breathe, and gain the serenity to speak again. It is not an intellectual emptiness or a bodily emptiness: it is a need to pause to calm your emotions.

This is precisely what silence is for. It is a moment of choice to react differently.

**Logorrhea exhausts thoughts.**

Have you ever found yourself in front of someone who talks nonstop about things that are often meaningless, empty of content? We end up with our brains confused, simply because we cannot keep up with the profusion of sentences. What if we are ourselves talking non-stop, tiring, and irritating people? Consider this and learn to be silent.

## What does silence say about you?

Silence makes the person who assumes it particularly striking. The one who takes time for silence seems to be in control of time, unlike those who talk non-stop, in a hurry, demonstrating a lack of self-confidence. We reiterate that silence is not an intellectual vacuum. By being quiet, you have more control over situations. Therefore, you will be more engaged and more relevant to the people around you.

## Knowing how to silence the voice, the body, and the mind.

It is not easy to be silent. Especially when we are involved in difficult situations, fierce discussions, or angry dialogues. We speak through words and gestures, and emotion is generated by the whirlwind of ideas that fills our minds. Failing to say something can seem humiliating to us, so we keep talking and generating discussions filled with arguments to come out as winners in everyday workplace or family debates. Generally, at the end of these clashes, we feel defeated and tired: we lose our peace of mind and, above all, our patience.

While words are commonly considered powerful weapons, silencing our voice, body, and mind is the best instrument to sow well-being, with ourselves and with others.

There are many areas of knowledge and activities that work with the potential of silence. In certain communities, it is used as a form of exclusion. Through it, you can ignore people, isolate yourself from the collective, and detract yourself from expressing opinions. Studies in anthropology that research the masquerades of popular revelries in Pernambuco explore the power of silence in carnival games (COSTA, 2009).[1] The masks hide the faces of the costumed players, who circulate around homes, streets, and squares, within the crowd that gathers to experience the carnival party. In this dynamic, the silence of the masked people is an active and significant element to preserve anonymity. The entertainment is found precisely in not talking, so that no one can recognize who is behind the mask.

---

[1] COSTA, Maria das Graças Vanderlei da. *Os Caretas de Triunfo: a força da brincadeira*. Recife: the author, 2007.

Masked people play the game of seduction, using their body as an instrument to make themselves seen. In these revelries, the speech of the body and the sound of silence is witnessed. No words are said, no voice articulation is heard: just a deep silence, wrapped in the sounds of the carnival party. The eyes shine under the masks through the small holes, which are windows of emotion. Silent, the players speak through gestures, creating an efficient communicative channel with the spectators: a game that mixes charm, fascination, and attraction.

As highlighted by Le Breton (2007),[2] the body is the object of representations, a semantic vector through which the relationship between us and the world is built. In the case of the games of masked people from Pernambuco, silence enhances anonymity by excluding a strong trait of our identification: the voice. It incites curiosity and causes symbolic bonds to be built, marked by the guessing game. Silence seduces and the mask makes this game possible.

In the field of psychology and psychoanalysis, silence is a working tool that is recognized as an important technique in clinical intervention processes. Having nothing to say in therapy sessions can incite fear in patients, but it often offers a path to happiness and healing.

In the context of religiosity and in areas where being introspective is essential, such as in

---

[2] LE BRETON, David. *A Sociedade do Corpo*; 2.ed. translation by Sonia M.S. Fuhrmann. Petrópolis, RJ: Vozes, 2007.

meditation and yoga activities, silencing the mind becomes an essential and indispensable factor. Through workshops and meetings to experience silence, one tries to listen to one's own thoughts, or even to silence them, so as to reach moments of reflection and self-knowledge.

By practicing silence, we start to listen to the other and create paths to understand what is being said. We also allow our interlocutors to hear their own voice and reflect on their positions and on our silent posture. This behavior often generates some discomfort and allows the other to also slow down the pace of their own speech.

Silencing speech, gestures, and the mind is not easy. There are many phrases that extol the importance of this attitude: "being quiet to listen to the heart"; "train the mind, by silencing it"; "listening to the silence, calming the soul"; and "silence allows self-control and discipline." We present silence as a catalyst for patience. From this perspective, the voice, gestures, and mind need to be silenced in unison to achieve patience. This is a complex movement as it requires attention and dedication. It is possible, but it depends on the effort of each one. While silence requires patience, silence is also one of the foundations of patience.

## The silent people and their attitudes.

Quiet people are not necessarily shy. They are calm, they have their own rhythm, and their own time and needs. For them, the world moves too fast, not allowing them to calmly analyze every detail in the face of the turmoil that surrounds them. Each nuance of their reality must first pass through the filter of emotions, and such delicacy, such meticulousness, takes a while to be reflected in their language and their art of living. Introverts are not comfortable being the center of attention. This style of behavior can cause a certain strangeness to the eyes of others, and the quietest people are often labeled as shy, suspicious, reserved, or individuals with a lack of interest. However, this personality type hides its treasures. In general, we perceive some basic characteristics in the most reserved and silent people: they think before they speak; they control their emotions, their impulsiveness; they are cautious when communicating; they know how to listen; they reflect on what they hear; and they need time to respond to what they are asked. Quiet people are often characterized by a certain self-confidence. They are not swayed by the opinions of others, and they have solid values and clear ideas. All these qualities leads them to cultivate full patience. In the end, the most silent are accomplices of the wisdom that comes from reflection and imagination and, above all, from peaceful silence.

## Silence in the art of suspense.

"I was walking down the street and that's when..." (Pause. Silence). This silence makes the interlocutor dive into expectation, into the excitement of waiting. "She was so..." (Silence). This is the effect of suspense. In colloquial terms it is a "cliffhanger": the idea that your audience is hanging off a cliff. In fact, they hang from your lips, and what awaits them below the cliff is the revelation you are about to make. For storytellers and comedians, the use of silence as a suspense creator is an important working tool, and it is the basis of a successful narrative.

## How long should we be silent in a moment of impatience?

For the question "How long should we be silent when impatience arises?", the answer is quite simple: performing all the steps of the "four friends" exercise requires four minutes. During this time, do not say a word. This mainly refers to the unpleasant family event mentioned earlier. If you are in a work environment, for example, it is almost impossible to spend this time quiet. However, if a person asks you for something, try to redeem that time by asking them "to wait only four minutes." Try to concentrate for one minute on each proposed "4S" exercise. Remember that everything is an exercise, a learning experience. When an unpleasant occasion arises, accept it as an opportunity to exercise and promote your self-control.

### Silent people—silence and personality.

Every day, teachers and educators are faced with students who spend the entire class in silence, sitting in the back rows of the classroom or secretly doodling in their notebooks. They do not like to answer questions aloud or interact in lessons. However, educational centers, and even universities, continue to value students who participate, who raise their hand and demonstrate enthusiasm and interest.

The stereotype that links extroversion to success or effectiveness remains ingrained in our mindset and society. The profile of the person who is extroverted and charismatic but at the same time egocentric and not necessarily sensitive to the needs of others continues to grow strong in professional contexts and in political elites.

It is as if the collective ideology values these behavioral and personality traits as effective without actually considering the productive performance or the ability to create an ambient of harmony between work groups. However, current research on leadership shows that people who are introverted, quiet, reflective, and patient have a much higher performance and foster a more pleasant human environment.

Leaders with an introverted personality profile do not currently predominate. They are strange beings in a world where extroversion continues to triumph. However, in professional contexts where a management group has leaders with a calm, reflective, and sensitive style, it is easier to leverage the skills of employees and work relationships.

Controlling silence at work improves quality of life and internal and external conflicts. Employees are much more proactive, more creative, and happier with an introverted, calm leader, as such a leader brings them confidence and new opportunities.

Quiet people often go unnoticed. It is seldom considered what lies behind their serene, demure, and silent appearance. They are usually observers and explorers of the senses who connect more intensely with reality and perceive the small details.

Each of us processes information differently. However, sometimes we ignore that these differences are mainly linked to our own personalities.

On the one hand, some people talk like a tornado, using 300 words a minute. Such people may find it difficult to be quiet and listen to themselves or others. On the other hand, some people find it easy to be silent and listen. This is usually a positive characteristic, because silence allows us to underline our qualities of control and the experience of full patience.

Silence is a powerful and invisible weapon. It is important for you to ask yourself if your own silence makes you uncomfortable. It is up to you, therefore, to understand the true quality of this friend and to know how to use it for your benefit and that of others.

**"Silence is the element in which great things fashion themselves."**

This understanding is true for a simple and fascinating reason. Every stimulus in the brain of an introverted person follows a complex pathway linked to emotional memory, analysis, and planning. Alternatively, more extroverted people have a lower tolerance and a greater sensitivity to stimuli, and therefore, they quickly launch into an impulsive response in the face of impatience. Although most of us have traits of both these types, we are closer to one of them. We need to know ourselves better, with full awareness of our actions.

# | SIGH |

# | SIGH |

"Then you let out that sigh,
that seems to unburden the soul."

*Caio Fernando Abreu*

In addition to silence, other remedies can be used against impatience. Since it is fundamentally born from an inadequate demand brought about by the activities and people that surround our lives, we must increase our capacity to welcome events as they happen and try to understand others as they are.

Cultivating contentment does not mean being indifferent but being serene in the face of novelties and unforeseen events. In short it entails being more attentive and calmer. Achieving this goal is a process. We need to prepare ourselves physically and emotionally against impatience, as it is an oppressive force that affects our body and mind.

Do you ever feel like you are tied down or out of breath when impatience sets in? When this happens, try to breathe more deeply and slowly to prevent impatience from taking a harmful toll.

First, the friend silence took care of you. The second step is to take care of your breathing. The sigh, the second "S" of the four "friends of patience" technique, offers good teachings for healthy breathing.

In situations where you find yourself to be impatient, such as in a traffic jam, breathe peacefully through your nose, lower your tense shoulders, look around at the spectacle of the world and the variety of human faces that exist around you. Impatience makes us suddenly get into unpleasant situations. By learning to slow down and giving priority to breathing and reflection, we can be attentive to what each person and each moment brings us.

## Practice breathing.

Take every moment of impatience as an opportunity to focus on your breathing and to reorient yourself. Straighten yourself, supporting your body with your feet or your chair. Breathe deeply as you observe your inhalations and exhalations, preferably through your nose. It does not take much time, just a few minutes.

Impatience is a physical reaction. When we are impatient, one or more of the following reactions occur: our heart rate increases, we run out of energy, or our muscles contract. When impatience overwhelms you, try to breathe consciously and divert your thoughts from this sensation surrounding you.

You can practice these short intervals of focused breathing several times a day, even when you are not feeling impatient. This is one of the pillars of mindfulness meditation. If you can breathe during calm moments, it will be easier to apply breath focus when you are feeling impatient.

**Here are some exercise ideas to practice breathing applied to mindfulness:**

- Focus your attention on your breath.

- Rest for 10 minutes in a calm environment and observe it. Feel the air go in and out through your nostrils.

- Breathe calmly while paying attention to the present moment: common activities such as walking, bathing, and eating are opportunities to practice mindfulness.

These small exercises allow us to slow down and become more present and develop controlled breathing.

**"Do not be impatient.
Happiness is not always
far from us."**

Happiness can often be much closer than we think. However, the impatience of trying to conquer it at any cost can blind us and prevent the realization from coming naturally. A good way to relieve such momentary pressure is to breathe through your nose. As we breathe, we relax and become calmer and more serene.

Inhale for four seconds and exhale for eight, repeating as many times as necessary. We quickly notice that our heart rate slows and our muscles relax.

As a result, we are also more successful in distancing ourselves from uncomfortable situations and heavy memories.

In relation to the importance of breathing, the second friend is the sigh.

## The sigh: a reinforcement.

Breathing is a continuous and commonplace act. It is mostly done involuntarily and without an effective awareness of the physical process involved. It represents life, survival, and health.

We sometimes hear this advice: "calm down, take a deep breath." This request comes when we are visibly stressed, agitated, or impatient. In such moments, we realize the importance of keeping an eye on this source of energy and tranquility. Breathing is consciously triggered at specific moments, such as during labor, to minimize pain and assist in the contraction process to facilitate the birth of babies.

In meditation practices, we focus on our breath, an instrument to draw attention to the present moment, by emptying the mind and relaxing the body: a time to pause and pay attention. In yoga, the breath amplifies the control of vital energy, called *prana*, which is essential for physical and mental balance. Physical exercises are also combined with breathing, which increases the performance of practitioners.

Linked to the breath, sighing is when we inhale and exhale deeply at different times of the day in a noisy and remarkable way. This is a common act when we feel tired or impatient and need to breathe in a different way that somehow catches our attention and that of others.

With a sigh, we reinvigorate ourselves to continue some activities and continue our daily confrontations. It is a special breathing through which we activate something necessary and effective for our health. By quickly filling and emptying our lungs, we increase the entry of oxygen into our body. In this short interval we strengthen and relax. Through the sigh, it is as if we revitalize the body and mind with a necessary outburst. In this manner, the sigh is a re-inforcement that increases our patience.

### How long to practice breathing in mindful-ness: a long sigh?

You can practice this breathing exercise for 1 minute in silence. Breathe slowly, but deeply. Slow, controlled breathing has been used for decades to promote mental calm. In medical practice, it is used to suppress states of overexcitement, such as panic attacks. However, the physiological mechanism of the relationship between slow breathing and brain activity related to this feeling of calm has not been fully scientifically studied.

**We can take the opportunity to learn more about breathing.**

One technique used in yogic breath control is *pranayama*. It exists in various forms, such as double, single, or alternating nasal breathing. Abdominal breathing, forced breathing, and vocalized breathing during singing are performed at varying rhythms and depths and are examples of *pranayama*.

Quiet, deep breaths can be set at a slower rate than the typical rate of 12–15 breaths per minute. They are usually around less than 10 cycles in normal adults, sometimes as many as six breath cycles in 60 seconds. This low respiratory rate maximizes heart rate variability by modifying respiratory sinus arrhythmia, a natural and beneficial phenomenon whereby heart rate increases during inhalation and decreases during exhalation.

Giving importance to inhalation and exhalation through the nose is an exercise in well-being, an exploration of the present moment and of each breathing movement during a moment of impatience. Considered fundamental to the development of physical well-being, this controlled, slow breathing is a form of meditation in itself and a preparation for the control of full patience. Do you breathe through your mouth or your nose while doing an effortless activity?

Slow breathing through the nose offers an exceptional breathing technique to calm and focus the mind as it helps to bring it back to the present moment. Focus your attention on your nose and the air that passes through your nostrils. If your thoughts begin to divert to other things, return to the present moment and to your attention to breathing.

Often, this movement of introspection, activated by silence and breathing, affects people and occasionally causes them to burst into tears. If that happens, it is no problem. You are on the right track. Tears are simply a form of expression, an outlet for feelings and emotions. Proceed with the "smile" and the "sure" to end the mindfulness exercise.

# | SMILE |

# | SMILE |

"Whoever wants to win in life
should do as the sages did:
even with a broken soul,
have a smile on your lips."

*Dinamor*

**The third "S" in the "4S" rule is the smile.**

After silence and the sigh (breathing), the smile can come into play. People often ask us where we get all our energy, our strength, our daily zest for life. We tend to sketch out stereotyped responses, generic arguments that we do not really think much about. At a certain point, we realized that the smile is a catalyst for good feelings and a generator of a good impression on the people around us. When we recognize the power of our smile, we understand better many of our reactions to life's adversities.

Imagine it is raining and you awkwardly hide under your umbrella and quicken your pace to buy time. Then you find someone who smiles at you: a careless act of a good father, who also has his own worries. You smile back and notice that his coat is completely soaked, so his child does not get wet. This chance meeting and the simple exchange of smiles gives you a pleasant feeling. It is calmness flowing like a waterfall, and suddenly the sky feels less heavy.

In another moment, you are near your house at dusk, tired and waiting for the light to turn green so you can finally get home. A fraction of a minute is enough for you to exchange a smile with the person in the next car, who is also waiting for the traffic lights. The wait seems lighter, and this act of cordiality is comforting for someone who has had a stressful day. Do you remember your college days, riding home on a crowded bus? A few sympathetic smiles from other passengers would bring a certain warmth: a feeling of compassion shared between strangers.

Many simple stories could be described here, and they would certainly elicit fond memories of this exchange of energy between acquaintances and strangers through a simple smile.

Human were made to smile—to smile at life and unforeseen events, surprises, your sadness, and your joy. Smiling at all stages of existence gives a sweeter flavor to your problems. When do you believe your life will give you continuous rest, with no problems in sight? This is a nearly impossible situation. There will always be issues to resolve, people who will snap at you, and painful issues to deal with. However, we believe that there is an advantage in facing life with positivity: the smile is a perfume with a soft fragrance or a spice with a special flavor.

We recognize that life is sometimes difficult. Not everything is joy, and there are bitter moments as well as anguish, fear, sadness, and pain. All this seems unbearable for us, and we would like to erase these heavy marks from the design of our existence. In light of these trials, try to smile. Assume this attitude; think about happy things, past and future; remember funny memories, the obstacles—even the painful ones—you overcame, the paths you have traveled and conquered so far; and have fun. By doing so, everything will feel much lighter.

Let's start exercising the use of this significant instrument for good living: the smile. How about smiling more on the street? Laughing outright when you think of something funny? Not hesitating to share joy, even if someone looks at us with a surprised and disconcerted stare? Trust me, they will not berate you, they will just be pleasantly surprised and smile back at you.

The fact is, we live in pursuit of happiness. As it cannot be permanent, draw fleeting moments with traces of pleasure: on the street, on the subway, on the bus, at the restaurant, in line at a store, at the bank, at work, at home—everywhere. Focus on giving smiles and receiving them.

At first, this third "S" may be difficult to apply. How can we smile when we are trapped in the labyrinth of our impatience?

It all comes down to exercise and belief: experiencing good moods and trying to focus on the here and now. Strengthen your conviction on the importance of self-control and the use of a smile as a key to minimize the consequences of the adversities that arise in everyday life.

Smile to yourself and to others. Receive the smile and know how to return it. Sow good humor and reap the fruits of more pleasant relationships. Believe that there is goodness and solidarity in the world and that interpersonal relationships can be improved, sometimes with just a smile. Start smiling and get used to it. You will surely reap good results.

## The art of smiling.

They say that art aims to represent the fluctuations of the soul: feelings and passions. Such expressions of mood and spirit have the smile as an ally. This singular movement, which brightens the face, brings with it some problems, as it can express feelings that are sometimes quite contradictory. There are many smiles that a human face can wear, including spontaneity, joy, sarcasm, malice, or shyness.

Artists are continually trying to understand and use the smile, because it is the symbol that best summarizes and illustrates the complexity of the palette of human emotions.

Painted around the early 1500s by Leonardo da Vinci, the Mona Lisa's smile has since fascinated viewers to the point of being considered the reason for her fame.

Throughout history and on different occasions, smiles reveal a lot about people. Smiling has become a cultural and social interaction.

At a time when the emergence of new technologies makes it possible to communicate via "emojis" (emoticons), we use the stereotyped yellow smiley-face to express feelings. Are we smiling less often in the real world and thus using these images to interact in the virtual world?

What matters is that we still believe in the power of the smile as a true human expression and a bridge between people. It is a friend whose value must be emphasized in the fight against impatience and in the art of living well.

## Smiling: vibrating with optimism.

Dawn. We open our eyes and go over the day's agenda. Generally, many activities await us: studying, work, family commitments, sports, leisure, emails, communication on social networks, religious meetings, medical appointments—a constant coming and going to deal with many obligations. We need to be patient to face the day that has just begun, to deal with different people, and to perform many actions, usually in a limited time.

When we wake up in the morning, we can choose to proceed from two different attitudes: start the day experiencing agony, a bad mood, irritation, and stress from thinking about facing a schedule full of activities, or we can choose to smile and be thankful for another day that starts, bringing with it the opportunity for both struggle and growth. Our choices can lead us to paths of pessimism and restlessness or to a path focused on well-being and patience.

How about we start the day with a powerful smile? The smile is therapeutic; it is healing; it is communication and interaction; it is simple and full of meaning. This facial expression can often seem banal, even involuntary, as a simple response to positive, funny, or pleasurable matters. However, smiling is much more than that: it is vibrating with optimism, and it is holding a key that opens doors, benefiting relationships and enabling exterior and interior growth.

A good mood, combined with a smile, works as a physical and mental movement that can help with social interaction by strengthening communication situations and helping you to cope with your emotions. According to Jean-Paul Sartre,[3] emotions are of paramount importance for psychic and social life, and they influence our "being-in-the-world." We seek meaning in emotions by looking for purposes and functionalities for our emotional behaviors.

We deal with reality daily. There is a life to be lived, problems that need to be solved, and relationships that need to be managed, and it is more salutary for all of this to be faced patiently. According to Sartre, emotions carry a certain magic that helps us apprehend the world in a special way, because through emotions we re-define our own lived reality.

---

[3] SARTRE, Jean Paul. *ESQUISSE D'UNE THEORIE DES EMOTIONS* - translated by Paulo Neves. Porto Alegre: L&PM, 2007.

Based on this idea, we believe in the strength of the smile as part of a foundation to build patience. A smile floods the body and mind with substances full of positivity and hormones that directly interfere with physical and spiritual aspects.

We do not intend to treat the smile as something commonplace, false, or forced. We believe in it as a sincere expression that helps us to vibrate positively, in an optimistic way, being an instrument that facilitates better relationships with the world and with ourselves.

## The true smile.

A smile is a human expression that can convey many different types of emotions. There is, among others, the fake smile, the fearful smile, smiles with the mouth open or closed, and smiles showing teeth or not. There are many possibilities. Try to pay attention to the types of smiles you use in your everyday life.

Faced with many ways to smile, how can we decode it as a reflection of the body and feelings?

Usually, an authentic smile is defined as the expression of a real positive emotion (e.g., joy, fun). When we smile, we activate muscle patterns: automatic, invisible micro-contractions that occur in the facial muscles that express our emotion. The expression of emotion then comes from an internal feeling that activates these micro-contractions or from a brain processing of the motor commands sent to the muscles.

The authentic smile has been named the "Duchenne smile" after the 19th-century French neurologist who deciphered it. It has the particularity of involving only the zygomaticus major muscle and the orbicularis oris muscle. "Smile with your eyes" is a label of authenticity, because the muscles in the upper part of the face, unlike those in the lower part, are not activated if the smile is forced.

The smiles that show greater spontaneity are characterized by a relative symmetry. However, they are not identical, and they vary according to the situation. Alternatively, the dominating smile is asymmetrical and is usually accompanied by a raised eyebrow.

The smile perceived as the most authentic involves all the muscles of the face. In addition to the eyes and the lifting of the corners of the lips, it involves a slight opening of the mouth. Try to trigger all this consciously, starting from your inner strength and your interest in cultivating patience. When you smile in this way, your smile will become more spontaneous and genuine.

In addition to the muscles of the face, teeth are also important elements of the smile. The more instinctive the smile, associated with a feeling of joy, the more the teeth will be exposed. However, this sign can be misleading when the exposure of the teeth denotes a somewhat "animalistic" smile, which can generate fear or express a desire for domination.

Until the 18th century, smiling with one's teeth bared was frowned upon. Only the poorest and most uneducated people engaged in such rudeness. This is proof of how smiles vary over time and across cultures. While in the West people spend fortunes in search of perfect white teeth, in Japan women look for dental clinics to have their teeth made crooked. For the Japanese, crooked teeth give people a more "youthful" appearance, making them more beautiful.

Can we fake a smile? In theory, yes. These muscles can be contracted voluntarily and consciously, without this being underlined by a necessarily positive emotion. However, this requires active effort, and the smile can appear fake. It is necessary to fight against the "enemies of patience," but using the "friends" to their full potential requires daily practice.

As a rule, an emotion is not only expressed by the muscles of the face, and it involves other more or less controllable body components. Smiling while shaking your head from left to right, as if making a negative gesture, does not make much sense. It looks like a gesture of disdain or contempt.

Is faking a smile a solution to one's impatience problems? No. However, working on optimism, resilience, and good humor are helpful solutions. Such practice is good for your body and those around you. With practice and full awareness of your feelings and desires, you will become used to smiling naturally in the face of life's adversities.

We are not encouraging you to smile falsely but to try to change your attitude in the face of stressful situations. It is common to lose patience with family, children, and friends in various daily situations. It is interesting to learn to face these moments with the help of a smile and a milder and more positive attitude.

Smiling is also important, even if you are alone. The smile sends a positive message to your brain, and makes you realize that some problems are not so important to the point of making you lose control of the situation.

Find a reason to smile. Smile for yourself. Smile because you love someone who is involved in the situation that makes you impatient. Smile because you have realized that you can control your mind and your impulses. It is a smile of gratitude to life, of self-control, of forgiveness, and of resilience—a smile of patience.

We have seen many elements that involve the simple act of smiling. Next, we would like to reflect on an important aspect: the interpretation of the smile also depends on the context. Interpreting smiles will also make us better understand the next friend of patience. During a TV gameshow, the loser's smile may have an almost identical shape to the winner's, but both will be perceived differently by the participants. Usually, the loser shakes their head in a negative way, like a "no," while the winner marks their smile with positive body signals. This leads us to a quick reflection on bodily aspects linked to the last "S," the SURE, another friend that can help us develop patience. We will see below how this last friend of patience works.

**"Whoever wants to win in life
should do as the sages:
even with a broken soul,
have a smile on their lips."**

Happiness can often be much closer than we imagine.

However, the impatience in trying to achieve it at any cost can blind us and prevent the achievement from coming naturally.

We believe that positivity opens doors, carves paths, and builds resilience, and it is an important factor for us to continue facing suffering and fears with determination.

# | SURE |

# | **SURE** |

"Don't tell me you can't.
There's a world that's just waiting
for you to say yes!"

*Tony Meléndez*

Moving your head up and down is a simple yet beneficial body expression for everyone. What tradition is more universal than the vertical nod for approval and the side movement for denial? What is the origin of these gestures? Are they really universal? In fact, no one really knows. We do not have clear answers about this, but we can reflect that, often, simple and common gestures have great acceptance and strength in different cultures. These examples are proof that the most trivial questions are not necessarily the simplest!

The "bodily" yes is a form of acceptance, in the same way that the no, expressed only by the movement of the head, reveals negation. Moving your head to say "yes" or "no" are gestures recognized worldwide. Any child recognizes and respects these basic principles. However, these rules are not so universal, which is contrary to what one might think.

## Meaning of acquiesce.

In most countries of the world, to say "yes" you nod your head up and down, and to say "no," you move from left to right. However, this is not the case in all the world. In Albania, for example, it is the opposite: they shake their heads from left to right to say "yes" and from top to bottom to say "no." If you plan on visiting Albania one day, pay close attention to the habits that have been anchored in you, otherwise you might end up saying "yes" when you want to say "no," and vice versa. Moreover, Albania is not the only country that practices this inversion. Bulgaria, Turkey, and Romania also use movements contrary to what we are used to. This difference comes from the time when there were Greek priests in churches. In Greek, "yes" is pronounced "*neh.*" In Bulgarian, "*né*" means "no." So when Greek priests said "yes" by nodding, Bulgarians understood "no," and consequently speech was associated with gesture.

In India, they shake their heads to acquiesce, tilting it from left to right. This move can seem confusing to Westerners, who translate it as "maybe yes, maybe no," or "more or less."

Other gestures also differ in other cultures. In Japan, the gesture to call someone is a movement of the hand facing the ground, moving back and forth, which is easily interpreted by Westerners as "go away." In any culture, some gestures are interpreted almost unconsciously, as they are part of a vocabulary of the body.

Although there are exceptions, as we have just seen, specific cultural aspects that can be found in some countries, and most people still decode the up-and-down nodding as a gesture of positivity.

### How many times should you shake your head and at what speed?

We are not going to change our magic number. Four should tell you something. Shaking your head four times, slowly, should be enough for you to assert your desire for personal control. The "sure" concludes the exercise of full patience. You will feel better knowing that you can continue to make your life choices regarding impatience. If you are in a heated discussion, you will express a certain positivity through this posture. It is as if you open a door for dialogue or even for a joint solution to a problem.

Movement speed is a measure of patience (or impatience). A slow nod shows interest in what is being said. Ideally, one person will respond with slow, paused nods while the other develops their arguments. Alternatively, quick movements make the speaker understand that we have heard enough and that we want them to finish or to let us talk.

It may seem that we are over-detailing the rules to better use this last friend, but it is of paramount importance as a catalyst for patience. We do not realize how much this affects us. We know, however, that body expression in full patience is an indicator of resilience. In the field of psychology, resilience is a person's ability to deal with their own problems, overcome obstacles, and not give in to pressure, whatever the situation. Theory says that resilience is the possibility for the individual to choose paths when they have the chance to take an attitude that is correct, and at the same time they are afraid of what this may cause. Resilience demonstrates whether or not a person knows how to function well under pressure. The resilient person adapts better to changes, and patience is a good instrument for us to reach this level.

## Yes is not simply yes.

Free will makes it possible to choose paths. There are several options for following good itineraries: studying, developing a profession, forming a family, cultivating friends, and making religious choices. Through these actions, we continue to be builders of our life.

Do we have the rudder of our boat? Most of the time we do, but the storms in the sea of life sometimes take us by surprise, and then we feel adrift, without direction, waiting for the tow to a safe harbor. It is precisely in these moments that we need to be patient and recognize that facing problems requires self-control and calm ways of finding solutions. Thus, we have the chance to choose to develop milder and more encouraging reactions both in the face of significant problems and in the face of small everyday acts that affect us and disturb our patience.

Therefore, we recognize the importance of a small gesture: yes. Through this subtle body movement, we have a powerful weapon that can help in our internal stability and in our external relationships. According to David Le Breton,[2] through their body humans place precise meanings in the world in which they are inserted, and bodily expressions are semantic vectors that express feelings. As social actors, humans relate to others using the symbolic systems determined by corporeality. Gestures refer to the actions of the body, which include the ways of consenting or denying that are expressed in the gestures "yes" and "no."

This primary gesture is socially constructed. From childhood, we hear educational words of positivity and negativity, and we see our parents reaffirm these "orders" with their bodies. Even before learning to express these terms through speech, the child repeats them through gestures that indicate affirmation or denial through simple head movements.

The gesture of "yes" represents a positive image, inducing the interlocutor to perceive a certain posture of calmness in the actor who is gesticulating. This consequently generates empathy and helps to reduce stress, both for the individual and for the collective group. In heated discussions, when someone nods positively, it gives the impression that they are understanding the other's behavior and ideas, based on their own impressions, assumptions, and understanding.

Does this gestural "yes" indicate an agreement with everything that involves and destabilizes us? Does it reveal a self-sacrificing attitude in the face of painful and hurtful circumstances? Not necessarily. "Yes" is not simply "yes." It is a choice to have a negotiating posture with ourselves and with others, rather than sealing an agreement of acceptance or conformism.

This simple gestural movement of the head carries a sense of reconciliation, bringing a certain comfort to those who perform it and to those with whom they dialogue. As Le Breton warns, gestures are loaded with meanings and values, and they actively insert humans into the social and cultural space, and the "yes" brings to the scene a fully positive and compromising attitude that helps to build the road to patience.

## Shaking your head is simply giving full consent to your decisions.

"Consent" expresses agreement, and it means giving permission for a certain act to be performed. Consent happens when there is a free will, allowing an attitude to be taken so that a certain end is achieved. It is a way of agreeing and giving approval to something or someone. By nodding, in a gestural way, the existence of assent or voluntary consent is assumed, which consists of the intellectual knowledge of the objective that is intended to be achieved. It also contemplates the practical will in relation to the means used to reach that same objective. Consent is fundamental to moral responsibility and gives authenticity to some acts, such as marriage, in many religions, where the consent of the spouses is mandatory.

The "Term of Free and Informed Consent" is a document used in the context of scientific studies with the purpose of providing information to a potential volunteer in a research. In social sciences, for example, such a document is signed by informants who participate in scientific research, announcing that they are aware of their participation and agree with the use of their information in the work, which may be published.

"Informed consent" is a common practice in current medicine, which consists of the legal and moral duty of the physician and the rights of the patient. It is a process in which the doctor provides information to the patient regarding a possible treatment or procedure. If the patient understands the information provided and demonstrates willingness to carry out the treatment, they signs the document, thus demonstrating their consent. If the patient considers that they do not want to undergo the treatment, they also sign the document, stating that they have been informed about a possible treatment that they have decided not to undergo. This way, if the doctor fulfills their duty to provide the necessary information, they cannot be held responsible if something happens to the patient, resulting from the treatment or lack of it.

Aside from the context of losing your temper, nodding your head saying "yes" serves two purposes. Since body language is also a subconscious reflection of emotions, a person who is affirming something tends to nod their head when speaking. Alternatively, deliberately nodding your head can help make your emotions positive. In other words, positive emotions trigger a nod, just as a nod triggers a positive state of mind. Moreover, nodding your head is contagious. When you see someone nodding "yes," you tend to imitate them, even if you do not agree with them. It is a valuable tool for bonding, gaining approval, or cooperating.

If you end each of your sentences with "is it not?" and by nodding your head for your interlocutor to do the same, you will provoke assertive emotions in them that will encourage them to seek agreement or dialogue. Say "yes" with your head while the other person answers your question.

We reiterate that nodding "yes" is a sign of approval. However, it is absurd to think that people who regularly resort to this mimicry might seem more docile and, consequently, less of a leader than others. Shaking your head up and down is not a posture of submission, and consequently, people who use this gesture during a conversation are no less dominant. As we have stated before, it is not a matter of agreeing with everything; it is simply a personal path of self-control: the recognition and acceptance that this situation needs your full patience.

The "yes" is a simple gesture and an effective way of saying to yourself, "I accept, I am free to consent and to react according to my choice and reflection." Do not be afraid to apply it, even when you are alone. Together with the other three friends, it sums up the reactions that we must employ to reach full patience in everyday life.

**"A moment of patience
can avert a major disaster.
A moment of impatience
can ruin a life."**

This statement might seem a little extreme. However, a person who has patience and knows the right time to act will be much closer to an assertive decision than one who gets carried away by the impulse of the moment.

# THE FOUR ENEMIES OF PATIENCE

**PEOPLE:** FAMILY, WORK, ACQUAINT-ANCES, AND STRANGERS

**TIME:** MOMENTARY OR LONG TERM

**SITUATIONS:** RESIDENCE, TRANSIT, SHOPPING, WORK, ETC.

**PEOPLE WITH A LACK OF TIME IN DIFFICULT SITUATIONS:** CHAOS

# | THE FOUR ENEMIES OF PATIENCE |

> "The key to everything
> is patience.
> You get the chicken
> by hatching the egg,
> not by smashing it."

*Arnold Glasow, American humorist*

Now that you know the solution to moments of impatience, we now address the four most common types of causes for losing patience.

**First and foremost**, we expect **people** to meet our expectations: we want them to act as we think they should.

*"The person in front of me should not act this way. It is unacceptable."*

*"If he told me he would call at 3 pm, he should call at 3 pm."*

*"This person on the street is not behaving like I think he should."*

Even if we think we are "right" because it is normal to expect politeness or honor commitments, in reality people rarely live up to our expectations.

**Second**, we tend to expect **time** to meet our needs, for example, we prefer no traffic jams, parking spaces close to our destination, no long lines, no delays at airports, and no long wait to be served at a restaurant.

**Third**, our expectations are usually unrealistic when we try to deal with what is happening in certain **situations**. We believe that we should be able to control all our thoughts and feelings as soon as they arise. However, "parasitic" thoughts and emotions are constantly arising. It is the nature of the mind to think and feel. Interrupting this process is as impractical as turning off the brain, and being impatient while we are dealing with different situations does not help at all.

Think about these three types of enemies of patience, and then try to identify if one of them tends to constantly appear in your life, or even all three together (which is the fourth enemy). This recognition will help you identify the moments when you react with impatience in the most diverse situations.

We highlight that when we bring the three enemies together, we usually lose control. Such situations involve the potent fourth enemy, **people short of time in difficult situations**.

Once you are able to sense your moments of impatience, try using the "4S" rule to help you deal with these situations. Think beyond your momentary frustration and ask yourself why you are feeling this way.

By doing so, you will start to detect which enemy is acting on your irritability. Create simple questions, like the ones below, and reflect on them.

**This slow, costly moment that you face, is it really decisive to the point of altering your joy?**

For example, a traffic jam or a crowded restaurant can make you feel irritated and frustrated. This is related to **time**.

**Are others not behaving the way you would like?**

For example, you might get impatient if there is another customer blocking the aisle of the supermarket or talking for a long time with the cashier. This relates to **people**.

**Cannot control your thoughts?** You can become impatient if you cannot control the thoughts and emotions that arise in your mind in a certain place, even though you know that there is not much you can do to avoid them. This can happen, for example, when you have to spend a day at a family member's house, because this is the schedule that your husband or wife has set for the family every year on a certain holiday. Impatience here is related to **situations**.

### Know how to detect signs of impatience in yourself.

The first step in dealing with impatience is recognizing this feeling within you. To do this, we can analyze our behavior and learn to listen to our bodies. What is happening to me? Am I tense? Why am I so nervous? What irritation does my state of impatience reveal through my exalted breath? You must learn to perceive these aspects yourself by noticing the signals your body gives. The body discloses our mood, and it is better to recognize it than to repress it or not give it attention. Like a snowball, a bad mood can grow and dominate us.

As we described at the beginning of the book, the main signs of impatience are the following:

**A**lways hurrying

**L**egs or feet shaking

**I**rritability

**O**utbursts

**T**ense muscles

**H**ard breathing

After noticing the signs, it is recommended to locate the causes of each impatient action. What or who is behind it?

If we try to observe ourselves for a few weeks, noticing the moments when we detect impatience, we will be surprised at all the insights and answers we gather. We will also be more aware and better prepared whenever that feeling arises again.

Through thoughts and questioning, we become aware of what causes our impatience. Doing so makes it easier to detect our enemies and trigger our friends, and thus, enable full patience.

Next, we describe learning ways of welcoming and delving into each enemy to expand our learning in this "battlefield."

After choosing silence, take four deep, slow breaths. Doing this will lower your heart rate, relax your body, and emotionally distance you from the situation. Smile and nod to accept the situation. Sometimes you may need a longer count or to repeat the process several times a day.

Force yourself to slow down. Speak and move more slowly. To others, it will appear that you are calm—and acting calm often makes you feel more patient.

Remember that you can choose how to react to certain situations. You can choose to be patient or not. The choice is yours.

Challenge your negative behaviors instead of letting your impatience build up. Try to remember the "4S" rule in the most difficult times.

Try to reframe circumstances in a more positive light. For example, people may not care if a meeting will be delayed as long as you let them know in advance that you are late. There may even be benefits to the delay, such as understanding a developing situation more clearly or reflecting on what you will face.

# | PEOPLE |

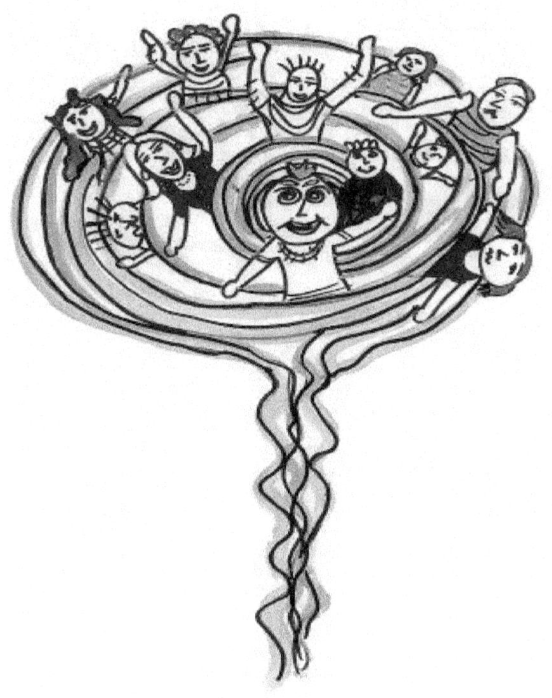

# | PEOPLE |

> "To be able to share
> in another's joy
> that is the secret of happiness."
>
> *Georges Bernanos*

To coexist means to live in close proximity or have cordial relations with someone. In our life, we deal with different people, in closer relationships or more sporadically. There are even fleeting encounters that also trigger our feelings of empathy or antipathy.

People are beings that circulate in our lives, leaving marks, nostalgia, joy, sadness, support, discouragement, and these emotions are linked to calm or irritation. Depending on how we weave these personal or occasional relationships, we build feelings and emotions.

If you are uncomfortable with a person, do not like someone, or cannot come to an agreement with someone, that is fine. What is the real depth of that feeling? Does the impatience come from you, or are you dealing with the other person's impatience and feeling hurt by it?

## Mirror, mirror, on the wall.

There are people who worry us. Often, from our first contact with someone, a feeling of discomfort invades us, and we cannot find answers to these feelings of antipathy that arise suddenly.

In our family circle, in professional practice, in the neighborhood, and in meetings with friends we are in contact with different people who manage, even unconsciously, to remove us from our comfort zone and destabilize our good mood. Sometimes what irritates us is their way of speaking or of taking a certain stance in a discussion. At other times, we criticize someone for their way of seeing the world, their values, and opinions. Even without asking deeper questions, we create a barrier in relation to the other, which distorts with our mood and makes us impatient. We build chasms between us and the individuals around us, and such preventions that keep us away from unwanted coexistence are often the result of unfounded unpleasant impressions, prejudice, pet peeves, or distrust.

When we momentarily stop to evaluate our feelings in relation to those who are part of our daily life or cycle of coexistence, we discover how intolerant we are in relation to those who are different from ourselves. From another perspective, perhaps what bothers us about the other are the actions and attitudes that are also part of us. It is as if we see our reflection in a mirror: we look at the other and, even unconsciously, we see in their unwanted characteristics that are similar to our own.

We need to be silent and reflect so we do not make hasty judgments. Being averse to someone we do not even know, judging their actions in advance, is like cultivating suffering for yourself, without any reasonable foundation. Judging those with whom we interact on a daily basis and with whom we have a close bond of coexistence amplifies moments of dissatisfaction through discussions. In fact, it is necessary to judge less: to silence the heart, making it more forgiving. Remember that judging others is often simply a way of talking about ourselves. We need to sigh and to focus our attention on the simple act of breathing deeply, an act that helps in the oxygenation of our cells. With this conscious act, be grateful for being alive and believe that you are a builder of happiness and change.

Try to smile more. Not that fake, mocking smile that keeps us away from people and ourselves. Plant the seed of joy and optimism, believing that we all have imperfections and are here to learn to grow collectively. Nature can be an exceptional example of renewal and beauty.

Accept your limitations and open your eyes to see others as companions on the journey. Say yes to the opportunities that arise through coexistence and confrontations. Reaffirm your awareness of the real importance of believing that we are part of a whole and that we are also as imperfect as those we judge.

Furthermore, practice these actions patiently.

**Tolerating others and the world:**

## expanding our vision.

*"The more the mind expands, the more patience grows."*

The word "tolerance" reminds us of one of the pillars of full patience, which is respect for the rights of others. This right is not only at the level of legality, but it also encompasses the right to exist, to manifest, and to be as one is. Anything that helps us to welcome the world and the other as they are will help us to walk the path of patience, helping us act against intolerance. Those who broaden their field of thought, following these itineraries, take a step forward, realizing that order and justice must reign in this world. Tolerance, acceptance, and respect are the keywords that should help us in this personal and collective work. The small events of everyday life offer us countless opportunities to practice.

First of all, consider the other's own rhythm: when taking care of small children or the elderly, we try to follow their cadence, adopting slowness. This thought must be extended to other people, if we are to respectfully observe their limitations and ways of acting.

Impatient people cannot bear imperfections, the limitations of things, the difference with oneself, or the similarity with what we do not appreciate in ourselves. Becoming understanding entails putting yourself in the other's shoes, accepting their strengths as well as their shortcomings, and reinterpreting differences as learning opportunities. In this way, we also learn to know ourselves.

We need to be attentive to learn to insert reflection between thoughts and actions. Patience begins with the time we give ourselves to not react quickly and thoughtlessly when something or someone bothers us. This time can be acquired using the "4S" rule.

Do you lose your temper if your child spills a glass of juice on the table or daydreams instead of tying their shoelace? Does your co-worker's work method irritate you because of their slowness? Faced with such everyday cases, we can try to reason, with full awareness, learning to cultivate a more indulgent and tolerant attitude in the face of the impulsive reflex of wanting to "explode" with impatience.

We must learn to deal with that which comes from the other and causes us some discomfort, especially when we are faced with situations or characteristics that we cannot change. It is important that we repeat to ourselves: let us be more patient with others!

We can do even better: objectively analyze our exalted behavior and realize that our first reaction was a manifestation of selfishness, related to the fact that we were confronted with an event that disturbs our routine and comfort.

Let us first determine if the problem is not in ourselves. "They invaded my territory, my comfort zone, they wasted my time, they upset my plans…" but is it really that serious?

It seems pretty simple, does it not? However, this has to be a broad and daily exercise. Therefore, we should listen to others without interrupting them. Let us try to understand what they are telling us and why they are doing it. Let us look for the positive aspect of that colleague's work method that irritates us so much. So we will see the positive side in all these situations.

Expanding the mind entails increasing the ability to welcome the other and the world, in addition to learning more about areas that are new to us. Accepting imperfection in things and people and then transforming that negative first impression into genuine concern for others can lead to the development of empathy, mindfulness in patience, and, ultimately, love. Love the reality around you with all its imperfections and all its differences. To love others, you need to love yourself and be ready for obstacles: it is a learning experience. Full patience is actually a form of self-love.

The secret of happiness is said to demand too much of yourself and too little of others. However, this requirement should not make us impatient to succeed and to be perfect to the point where we become intransigent or want to control everything and everyone. To be tolerant with yourself means, first of all, to recognize your imperfections and flaws. Accepting your own powerlessness is a good step on the path to self-knowledge. This helps us to discern our weaknesses to try and overcome them. This examination of ourselves and, in particular, of our impatient and intolerant attitude will help us to be more tolerant, benevolent, and resilient. We should observe the self, the other, and the world in which we are inserted.

## Being in relation:
## individual, collective, and universal.

There are three dimensions to the human being: the individual, the collective, and the universal. Initially, as a child, we gain awareness of our body, of our dependence on family members, and of contact with nature. Everything is a discovery and a learning process.

Years go by and we continue to add information and multiply knowledge. The awareness of our identity and belonging to places expands the world that surrounds us. Questions about the unthinkable and so many things that we do not understand also begin.

Objectives and survival paths appear: study, work, family formation. The conviviality is amplified, and we begin to perceive the existence of these three important conditions of the being. As individuals, we are unique, managing body and mind, matter and spirituality. As a collective, we create friendships, relationships, and connections that expand the connection and distance between the *I* and the *others*.

In addition to the understanding of the internal and external self, the feeling of the unknown and the unexplainable is added. We then go on to try to understand our position in the universe, the relationship between life and death, and the definitions between space and time.

New questions arise. Regardless of our religious option, we generally seek to find the answers to what we cannot explain in faith and in the relationship with the sacred. In this context, spirituality becomes an ally for us to be able to continue with everyday challenges.

Like a whirlwind spinning over time, we go through different situations, controllable and irremediable, predictable and unexpected, which disrupt and strengthen us. Our body and mind suffer the consequences of the intensity, good or bad, of the situations experienced and felt.

From this complex context that surrounds us, we have to understand how necessary it is to seek to strengthen our patience, not limiting ourselves to reliving episodes of the past or expecting future achievements. Memories and plans are important, and memories and dreams are essential. However, we need to learn to live today and understand that the present is drawn by the seconds that shape the clock of time: each grain that moves in the hourglass forms the cycles of life. We seek to be happy. We want to fulfill ourselves. We crave health and peace. We fight for material and spiritual achievements. Through patience, we strengthen the three dimensions: the self, our relationship with the other, and what connects us to the universal. This is not an easy achievement, but a necessary and pleasurable one when consciously pursued. We must be grateful for the daily exercise in the concrete and patient search for a formation of this *being in relation.*

**Full patience with people at work.**

Work is an environment in which we need to make important decisions all the time, and this makes impatience present in the desire for faster results. However, in most cases, good results do not depend only on ourselves but on countless variables and people. Since we are aware of this, it is wise to choose to control our emotions, to take charge of our breathing, to observe the silence inside and outside of us, and to act with positivity. In other words, we must be the true manager of our actions. This will require two fundamental skills: emotional intelligence and self-knowledge.

Interpersonal patience is full patience with other people, with all their demands and shortcomings, with any obstacles that may involve these relationships.

You may think of some people as slow learners, difficult to understand, or even somewhat irrational. They can have bad habits that severely frustrate us. However, losing patience with them is usually never beneficial, and instead, it can make the situation worse.

Patience and understanding are essential when you are hiring new staff or delegating tasks. It is also a great help in dealing with difficult co-workers or managers. It is essential for quality service to the client or their family members. In short, whatever the activity you carry out, you will have the opportunity to experience patience through sporadic contact or a more effective interaction with the other.

This kind of mindfulness is active. It requires immense effort to keep your mind sane and your body calm. Listening skills and empathy are vital, and when you are dealing with difficult people, you need the self-awareness and emotional intelligence to understand how your words and actions affect any given situation. You cannot simply wait and hope for the best; you have to build relationships that are stable, whether fleeting or lasting.

Why not take the opportunity to practice the rules of full patience by putting the four friends into action? Give the other person your full attention: silence yourself; take a deep, calm breath; smile; and respond with affirmations. Try to see beyond your own frustrations by imagining yourself in the position of the other who is being received.

Remember that impatience rarely has a positive effect—in fact, it can even interfere with a person's ability to perform. Impatience will likely generate more conflict and stress, which will be counterproductive. Becoming more patient will not happen overnight, but persistence always pays off!

**And if impatience is present in the other?**

In this case, the most important thing is to cast aside your judgments and to practice empathy. Putting yourself in someone else's shoes is a helpful way to understand what your friend or family member is going through and to find the best way to help them. Sometimes all someone needs is to be heard, to vent, and to talk about the causes of their lack of patience. By helping them, you will minimize the impatience that you may experience.

## Acceptance and people:
## full patience solutions

Allow emotions to be present without judging them. Practice naming emotions in a stable and relaxed way—"joy," "anger," or "frustration," for example, without these being labels loaded with limitations. Accept the presence of emotions without judging them and then let them go.

Above all, the practice of mindfulness involves accepting what arises in your mind in each moment. When you reflect on your experience during a situation where you tried to use the "4S" rules, it makes it easier for you to accept whatever comes your way for the rest of the day.

Acceptance is a pillar of full patience. Even if we want to cling to the edges of certainty, life is inherently the great unknown. People are mysteries. We are completely ignorant of what will happen to someone's mood, and this uncertainty of the future creates a certain fear and anguish. If this insecurity remains, it can turn into anxiety and take over our lives in different situations.

Likewise, it is disturbing to hold on to what we have experienced in the past to build our expectations for the future. In any case, even if our past actions have sown what we will one day reap, there is no guarantee that the harvest will be "good" or "bad."

Like time, life is surprising and capricious. Yesterday's bloom, which seemed to promise a beautiful harvest for tomorrow, can be destroyed in an instant by unpredictable hailstorm, an unexpected drought, or a devastating parasite.

In such situations, acceptance is essential. The awareness that there is no magic formula to change people's behavior, but only significant effort to improve yours, is a good way to start the journey. By training ourselves to choose patience at every moment, to release our minds from the aggression of impatience, to change our perspective on life, and to appreciate each day as it is, we learn to see our fears and uncertainties in a whole new light. We may even discover that the worst people and most stressful situations bring great teachings and contain treasures of love. Moreover, behind many of the sufferings there are wonderful rewards: maturation and personal evolution.

When considering things head on and from a certain distance, we observe that each difficulty hides an opportunity to grow, to learn, to change something, and to transform. What the caterpillar calls death, the butterfly calls rebirth.

In accepting things as they are, from a patient perspective, we find that behind the smoke veil of fear—fear of suffering, of being afraid, of failure, of knowing, of succeeding, of death, of facing difficulties, of change—there is another reality where life is hidden: in full patience.

Imagine that you are in physical or mental pain. Your body hurts or your mind is troubled. Would acceptance really be your first step? Would not your natural reaction be to try to ignore your unpleasant or painful feeling? Maybe you act like you do not feel anything or you try to change those sensations by distracting yourself. Some may even try to drown their suffering by drinking alcohol or taking medication or drugs.

This search for relief through evasive behavior will undoubtedly work in the short term. However, in the long term, these behaviors will not deceive the mental or physical suffering that will reappear, sometimes in an amplified way, as a predator devouring the body or the spirit. In the medium and long term, there will be a risk to cultivate vicious behaviors that conceal symptoms and do not solve the real causes of suffering.

We can feel an increase in pain. Then, gradually, you will build emotional and mental suffering around this pain that you seek to avoid, ignore, refuse, manipulate, and hide. All this will only aggravate and keep the phenomenon in a vicious cycle.

Often, we develop a whole internal discourse about these feelings until we make it our identity. Thus, we begin the arguments to justify the suffering. "I have no luck in life." "I am someone who has pain and who suffers." "I do not deserve to be well and happy."

In this perspective, we have created our own suffering body, this mental "entity" generated through a negative soliloquy.

An attitude of acceptance and resilience teaches us to know how to behave in the most appropriate way possible in the circumstances that bring us suffering. The questions of "What to do? How to act?" are means of recognizing the problem.

It is not an attitude of resignation or submission, nor is it a behavior that expresses passivity or abandonment. We need to allow our painful emotions to exist by observing them in the present. We have to reflect on what permanent, unexpected, and sometimes unwanted changes are happening in us and in our relationships.

Acceptance has nothing to do with passivity. On the contrary, accepting things as they are is a dynamic and proactive attitude, which considers the importance of giving space to what is present to make a choice with full awareness of how to respond to what is being presented.

The opposite attitude of not controlling, ignoring, or refusing unpleasant feelings, emotions, or thoughts can have dramatic consequences for personal balance in the long run. This attitude of denial or refusal—often unconscious—configures automatic behaviors and reactions that comfort us in the famous "zombie" mode. This mode of operation leads us to live blindly without valuing the sensations and feelings that are present or their precious messages to conduct our life in a fulfilling way. In this mode that opposes acceptance, we act almost systematically against our real needs.

With insight and acceptance, we discover that the feelings that accompany certain unpleasant experiences do not last forever and that everything is impermanent and eventually passes.

It is not easy to experience acceptance and resilience. It is a constant exercise and change of conduct.

To break the vicious cycle, we must redefine our internal thought system and install a new virtuous *software* so that acceptance becomes a daily practice. This is the key to move past guilt and stop vilifying and belittling yourself. It is interesting to start with the practice of mindfulness meditation. During mindfulness exercises, by observing the pains that exist in your body, the unpleasant emotions that invade your mind, and the thoughts that suddenly arise, you begin to experience the here and now, giving yourself time to practice the unconditional acceptance that is the basis of true love.

When your mind wanders, try gently to bring your attention back to look closely at that part of your body where there is pain. By noticing its existence, instead of running away or rejecting it, you can face it with kindness and recognize it: you give it space. A space in which it will dissolve, moment after moment, breath after breath.

At first, your feelings, emotions, and thoughts will interfere with the practice of meditation. In time, you will no longer seek to apprehend, reject, or modify what you feel, but will simply accept the feelings completely as they are. Such acceptance will be as an act of unconditional care and love for oneself. You will generate less suffering and feel much freer on a daily basis.

As scientific research shows, the perception of your pain will diminish to the point of sometimes disappearing completely for a while or a long time. Your pain resistance threshold will increase as you are able to identify your body's sensations. You will then have discovered the power to accept things and especially people.

## We do not choose our family: acceptance is a keyword.

From what age does a human being have the ability to start cultivating patience? The ability to wait significantly changes, depending on age. Before they reach one year old, a child still does not understand that they are a complete person, separate from their parents. Therefore, the distancing of their relatives generates insecurity in the child. Before the age of three, the child usually reacts intensely when asked to wait or to use patience, because they have difficulty understanding the point of view of another person who shows them the need to wait. Although you can get a child be used to being patient, but you need to explain in clear terms why you cannot respond to their request right away.

From the age of four, children understand the concept of patience and can tolerate waiting a certain amount of time before their needs are met. At this age, they are also more autonomous. Therefore, you can ask them to take care of themselves, at least for a short period. Some children are easier to deal with than others. Acceptance is the key word to better manage family problems, whether related to children or close relatives.

## How to react to your child's impatience?

If you are busy and your son is doing everything he can to get your attention, here is how to make him wait. Ask yourself if your child is seeking your attention to satisfy a real need or to satisfy an unimportant desire. A need, such as thirst or going to the bathroom, must be met immediately. On the contrary, wishing to satisfy a momentary desire can wait.

Avoid extreme reactions. Be silent. Look at him. Breathe. Smile and say yes. For a child, "yes" is important. When we are in autopilot, "no" is the first word that comes to mind, as a mechanism of energy saving and a reflection of individual self-protection.

Be careful! If you respond to the other's wishes too quickly, they will not learn to wait and adapt to time managing. Alternatively, if the wait is too long, your son might think you do not care about what he is saying. Listening to your child in these moments nurtures their dreams and makes them want to share them with you again.

Educating is not easy. Set boundaries and be consistent. Sometimes it may seem easier to close your eyes and meet requests, especially when the child is demanding or being uncompromising. However, acting in this manner can encourage a continuation of this kind of behavior for the rest of their life.

Be tolerant. A child thinks first of their own needs and desires. Therefore, it is normal that they ask for everything at all times and want answers as soon as possible. As a parent, however, you can make them understand that some of their requests are acceptable and others are not. Use routine to help your child understand their desire can be satisfied when it is safe and possible to serve them. For example, tell him, "Now I have to prepare the meal. I can hear your story while we eat. After the meal I'll put away the dishes and then play with you in the living room."

Value their ability to wait, and teach them how to tame anxiety and cultivate patience. You will give them the tools to live in society.

Although your child can predict a situation by observing family gestures, it is difficult for them to assess the length of the wait and how long they will have to manage their patience. Tell them why they need to wait and when you can respond to their request. This will make the wait more bearable. They will then understand that you have heard their request and that you will respond shortly. "I'll read you a story after I clean the kitchen." "Look, I'm washing the counter. Then I'll put the dishes away. I know you do not want to wait for me to finish, but I also know you can wait."

In this small example, you and your child will be exercising patience and building a friendly and trusting relationship.

## Patience transforms relationships.

Sometimes in our interactions, we become defensive, angry, and say something to hurt others. We do not realize the importance of patience and end up making rash decisions. Whenever you feel defensive towards someone, try to be calm enough to think about the positive qualities of the other person.

Disarm yourself. Put yourself in their place. Silence yourself and listen.

We reiterate that cultivating empathy with others is important if you want to live a life without complications. Patience helps us to accept others as they are and makes us tolerant. By being impatient, you suffer more and also make others suffer. Patience helps you to acquire a positive attitude. If you find that any life situation is challenging or difficult to bear, try to reshape that situation and see its positive side.

Did you know that full patience makes you healthier? Anger and stress are enough to ruin your health. Patience is the antidote to these two sickly feelings. Thus, you can overcome any challenging situation with more flexibility and in the best way. By being free from stress and cultivating calm and happiness, you will maintain a healthier life, physically and spiritually.

**"To be happy is to know
how to effectively manage the bridge
that separates patience from impatience."**

The size of this bridge varies greatly. The only certainty you have is that only with patience will you figure out what is at the other end.

Beware: this passage is fragile!

Running and performing brash movements can cause the bridge to break. Learn how to cross over, one step at a time, always reflecting. Be the builder of your learning process. Observe, review, ponder, and draw conclusions.

# TIME

# | TIME |

"Happy is the man who early learns
the wide chasm that lies between
his wishes and his powers."

*Johann Goethe*

Prepare to act in the face of long waits. Many people are annoyed when they are forced to wait too long, for example, in a particularly slow restaurant or in a doctor's office. If you can be distracted by other activities while waiting, it will be easier to stay calm. You can read a book, do a crossword puzzle, or be distracted by a pocket game. You can also have fun with whatever comes your way. Listen to conversations around you, watch other drivers stuck with you in traffic, or read the headlines of magazines and newspapers while you are in a queue.

Remember when you used to sit at school listening to the teacher talk for hours, looking at the clock and feeling like every minute was an eternity? You grew impatient, hoping that the bell would ring so you could finally get out and play. You felt bored, hoping that class would end and that you could do something that really interested you. If, instead of taking that course, you had chosen something you were passionate about, you would not have looked so much at the clock nor felt an endless wait. However, we often have to follow the middle road to reach future goals. Basic and boring disciplines are necessary to reach the targeted job.

Becoming bored is another way of saying that you are going through difficult times: we feel anguish and impotence. Like any unpleasant moment, we want the boring activity to end as soon as possible. In such situations, when we lose our patience.

Imagine someone, at rush hour, waiting at the bus stop. The school term had just begun, so there were many people there. To make matters worse, the subway was slow because there was a broken line two weeks ago. There were all the conditions to be impatient. Around you, people were writhing their faces, sighing, stamping their feet, and getting impatient. The message on the speaker said, "Our company wishes you an excellent return to school and a great day!" It was an out-of-touch message given the chaotic situation, and it was ironic. Soon, a person remembered a book he had read and began to apply the "4S" rule. His smile and the nodding of his head with a positive "yes" sign, began to infect some people who a few minutes earlier were tense. It was an ironic "yes," but it was unintentional, and the message of the smile had created an interference in the behavior of those who watched. They went from a feeling of impatience to a feeling of fun and interaction in the span of a few minutes. Creating an interruption is the fastest way to drown impatience. The best way to create these interruptions is to use humor. If we realize that we are becoming impatient, we can try to break that feeling with something that amuses us or makes us feel good. Smiling is a solution, and so is expressing positivity through your body. By taking the focus away from our impatience, we immediately find calm and serenity, in addition to infecting other people.

## A time we do not control.

According to Greek mythology, Cronos is the god of time. In Roman myths, Saturn, son of Heaven and Earth, is the deity who rules over temporality. Iroko, in African religions, is the Orisha of time, the one who governs ancestry.

In African culture and religion, time does not follow the linearity created by Western cultures. It is cyclical: what happens in the present or in the future has already happened at some point and was lived by the ancestors or by the Orishas. The Western conception of time follows a linearity, a line that guides us and also imprisons us in yesterday, today, and tomorrow. In turn, we often become prisoners of the events of the past or of the plans of the future, forgetting to effectively live the reality of the present.

What is time? A convention? Something real? An instrument of organization? A scientific concept?

Nature can be an exceptional teacher who shows us how to observe temporality, such as the beginning of day or night and the seasons that mark the passing of the year. Sun, rain, snow, wind, leaves, fruits, seeds, bird songs, the movement and mating of animals, high temperatures, mild or low ones, and colors that change all mark the seasons, filling them with perceptible signs and weather indicators.

Time is also witnessed by the phases of the moon, the position of the stars, and which ones are present in the sky. The marks and scars on our bodies also record the years of our existence.

Nature is an example, and we are usually distracted observers. We prefer to look at the instruments built by humans, even if they are mirrors of the teachings of nature. Clocks, cell phones, calendars, diaries, alarm clocks, and television programs incessantly guide our life, assisting in our movement and speed. We draw our sequence of tasks and continue to embark on the waters of time, often suffocating feelings so dear to our existence: calm, softness, tranquility, pondering, serenity, patience.

Living and coexisting. Working and creating. Producing and knowing. Developing countless activities, moving continuously. Everything is important and necessary. The contents of our lives are essential, but real wealth is in the way we choose to deal with the pulsation of things: the relationship between time and patience in this daily confrontation.

This narrative was being written from 2020 to 2021. It is interesting to discuss the characteristics of time and its consequences related to our patience in those years when the COVID-19 pandemic hit our planet and made us stop. We were forced to rethink the paths we built on the timeline, experiencing another way of dealing with the rush, the speed and the dynamism to which we were accustomed. We had to build isolation strategies as an instrument of survival.

Staying at home in confinement with close relatives; coexisting constantly with these relatives;

getting away for a significant time from our workplace and leisure activities; and abandoning practices that were part of our daily lives in sports groups, religious groups, or social activities. All this started to interfere directly in this new present time, affecting us physically, mentally, and spiritually.

A new time. A "new normal." Another way to create and recreate patience: with us, with others, with all the limitations, and with the relationship between life and death.

## Time is not equal to money.

Benjamin Franklin once warned a young merchant that "time is money." At the time in the mid-18th century, it was a meaningful guideline. Today, in many cases, people still think that this makes sense and is quite relevant.

In a capitalist world like ours, many live engaged in production, labor, profit, power, and accumulation of goods. The truth is that the saying "time is money" has put us in more trouble than we thought. Since we live within this deceptive premise, we try to do more in less time. We began to confuse activity with productivity, as if "doing" guaranteed "having," and then we forgot about "being." Inadvertently, we jump on the hamster wheel, running as fast as we can with a competitive mindset against the clock and what it supposedly represents.

Technological advances have come to improve many aspects of communication. However, the infiltration of devices such as computers and smartphones in our lives has transformed humans into prisoners of a time that runs differently, and everything is incessantly connected.

We have created a negative relationship with time, which gives us a sense of "time hunger" rather than abundance. Even our precious vacation time is not immune to the time-money equation as many people engage in work-related activities during the holidays. The trend seems to be increasing with smartphones and Internet access everywhere.

If you think you can never leave work to rest, you may need to consider a change in your lifestyle.

Your body will tell you if you are on the right track as it gives signals. Have you ever wondered why you feel so much better during vacations? Not only is your stress level reduced, but you also tend to eat calmer and sleep more. Your body is a barometer to know if your pace of life is working properly or not: it measures the pressure that surrounds you. Invest in a little slowness in your holiday routine and realize the pleasure you will receive. Cultivate your patience with the "4S" rule as well. A slower road is a great place to watch your surroundings! Use the time to get to know time and cultivate patience, and live in the present with more tranquility.

# SOLUTIONS IN FULL PATIENCE
# FOR TIME ISSUES

## Learning to remain in the present.

A less formal approach to mindfulness can also help you stay in the present time and participate intensely in your life. You can choose any task or moment to practice informal full patience, whether you are eating, bathing, walking, listening to a partner's speech, or playing with a child.

Animals have a lot to teach us. They are masters of full patience. They inspire us to embrace the present moment intensely. Dogs and cats are inspiring, and their minds are much calmer than ours. They do not torture themselves with yesterday's lost time nor with what will happen tomorrow. It is the wisdom of nature.

Although some dogs bark constantly, silence is always present when animals have no physiological needs. They breathe slowly, wait for hours for their owners to arrive, and are happy, smiling in their own way with a wagging tail. This gesture is their "yes" of positivity and joy. We can learn plenty from watching them.

Nature has its own wisdom. The time, the passage of days, and the seasons are felt with intensity and within all their "irrationality." Animals interact intensely with these changes. From the smallest insects to the largest mammals, humans can and must take advantage of these lessons, sharing with animals a different form of learning: to be an observer of what surrounds them and experiencing the present moment consciously.

We reiterate that focusing on the "4S" rule at a difficult time of impatience can be pleasant. It is as if there is a voice telling you "you are at level 10." An intense situation with a difficult person in that relatively long period of time will surely upset you: it will be impossible to hold on.

Then you remember the reflections we did together. It is a pleasure to have this sense of control when the impatience team tries to win the game. More so, the real pleasure is when we manage to pull the rope to the side of the "friends of patience."

**"Let us take our time,
but let us not waste time."**

*José Saramago*

Do you want to have a healthy life and a youthful appearance?

Then, avoid impatience.

Live your life with calm and tranquility.

After all, we do not know how long this life will be and how many changes can happen in our path.

So, what is the point of rushing?

# | SITUATIONS |

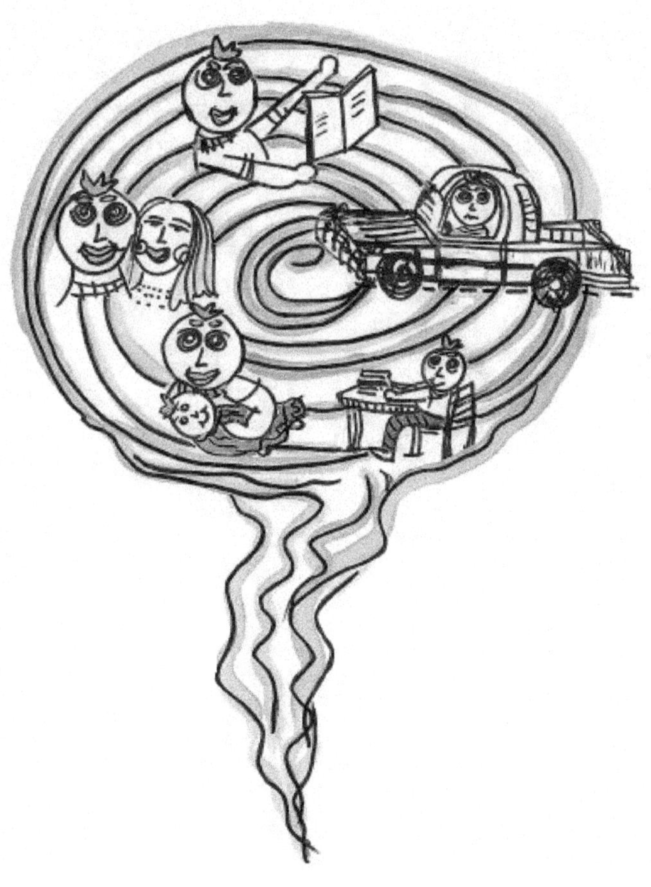

# | SITUATIONS |

> "Where we stand is not
> as important as
> the direction in which we are moving."
>
> *Oliver Wendell Holmes*

**D**o not blame yourself for the bad times.

If your impatience is the result of a frustration you feel with yourself, take a step back and realize the difficulties you are having in coping with certain situations. Reflect on how you can work around problems or turn them into something positive.

The impatience you feel is often a product of the preconceived idea that it is better to solve everything faster, which is not necessarily true. By going slowly and patiently, you will understand situations and people in more detail and in more depth, and you may even have fun doing so. Remember that it takes time and effort to become an expert at most things. Being patient with yourself is the best gift you can give yourself.

## Patience with life's hardships

We could use "perseverance" to summarize coping with life's difficulties with patience. To persevere means to be patient to overcome a serious setback in life, to have tolerance to wait for the outcome of a lengthy lawsuit, or to endure a difficult medical treatment. It can also include your ability to work toward a long-term goal—be it professional, such as a promotion, or personal, such as staying fit or saving for the holidays.

Whatever the obstacle you have to overcome, it will probably require determination and focus. You will need to keep your emotions in check throughout this process. Your emotions vary along the way, from anxiety to anger, including frustrations and discontent. All of this can cause you to become unmotivated. Proceed with perseverance and calm.

## SOLUTIONS IN FULL PATIENCE FOR PROBLEMS IN ADVERSE SITUATIONS

### Gratitude and detachment.

Detachment is another pillar of the practice of full patience. The power of attachment over the human mind is significant. It is at the origin of the strong emotional bonds that weave us together with other elements, both material or immaterial. These bonds become the reason for dependent, defensive, aggressive, and possessive behaviors. The feeling of attachment, therefore, generates fear, tension, and suffering. In difficult situations, such as in divorce, mourning, or an inevitable discussion, always use patience as a tool to maintain control and resignation.

Attachment and desire support each other in a vicious circle of co-dependence: the greater the desire, the more attachment grows, both for the object of desire and for the energy that desire generates in you. Therefore, renouncing the things or people that are dear to us presents a difficult challenge.

Who has not experienced a strong feeling of desire for something or someone? Do you remember, for example, wanting to have a house since you were a child? Feeding the idea of having a car, looking at images from all angles and wanting to make a thousand plans with it? We suffer when we have to "give up" that dream, and we experience for sadness at the idea of not having such an object at the desired moment. How can we learn from experiences like this? These are situations that provoke anxiety but bring valuable teachings for other adversities that may come. With lucidity and without excessive attachment, we can make choices that allow us to find solutions to certain problems. Being free from emotional attachment, we free ourselves from the desire to possess something immediately and the psycho-emotional dependence generated by that desire. Thus, we move forward on our way, free and happy. This behavior of patience and resilience helps us and helps those around us, such as family members.

When situations that elicit confrontation and resignation arise, first be silent, breathe, smile, and say yes to yourself. This process helps you to patiently learn not to "cling" to material things or people who arouse ideas, dreams, and feelings. Nothing lasts forever, and everything is constantly changing and we do not have control of all the situations that involve us. Change and the movement of life bring losses and require renunciations. If our attachment is too great and our desire for possession is too strong, any change in a relationship, occupation, or power becomes a great source of suffering on our journey. Instead, let go.

This does not mean that we should be insensitive and totally detached from emotion and affection towards the people and things that shape the situations around us. Practicing detachment does not mean a refusal to live and fully experience everything that happens in our lives.

To live fully and consciously, we must feel pain and compassion in the face of suffering, pleasure in good times, fear in frightening contexts, anger in unacceptable situations, and joy in moments of grace.

To practice detachment means to be aware that each of these situations, sad or joyful, is only fleeting, because nothing lasts forever. Instead of "clinging," we must understand this impermanence by harboring these feelings. Experience what there is to experience in the moment by being fully present and aware of the situations that are experienced.

What does that understanding have to do with patience? Simply everything. We become much more impatient when we are attached to things, to situations, and to our precious time in an attempt to seek maximum effectiveness. The deepest manifestation of the practice of detachment is a positive attitude towards all circumstances of life: having nostalgia for the past and hope for the future, but living the present with full patience. Thus, no matter what happens, our internal state tends to become more independent of external circumstances.

Wisdom consolidates detachment and comforts Full Patience. This reinforces unconditional love, which is the feeling of being connected and being one with everything.

**"Patience is the best weapon
to support all that
which does not depend on you."**

It is important to make an addendum: do not mistake patience with laziness, conformism, or stagnation.

Do not put off till tomorrow what you can do today, and especially what depends on you.

As for what is not in your control, all that remains is to wait or accept.

# | PEOPLE WITH A LACK OF TIME IN DIFFICULT SITUATIONS |

# | PEOPLE WITH A LACK OF TIME IN DIFFICULT SITUATIONS |

*"To avoid running out
of patience,
recharge it."*

We can become impatient in relation to a situation, someone, or time itself. When these three elements come together, straining our emotional instability and our physical and mental health, most of the time we lose control: we fall in chaos. This "enemy monster" is the fiercest, strongest, and hardest to fight. It is the enemy who is present in everyday life, in the accumulation of situations that provoke instability, in the time lost due to irritation, and in the challenges in personal relationships. It is when the brain "tilts" and breaks down, and like a player in a decisive match, we are completely stunned, not knowing how to identify what or who is responsible for the problem.

Identifying the "enemies of patience" one at a time can be quite easy and usually does not cause us to "burn out" from a loss of patience. However, when everything gets out of control and this fourth powerful enemy arrives, the quickest way to restructure is to implement the "4S" rule.

To get to know your four enemies in detail, try one observation so that you can think a little more about this complex universe. Do you remember when you became an impatient or even explosive person? By any chance, did you live with relatives who were nervous and ready to detonate, and you felt the stress of these people on your own skin?

A child often unconsciously reproduces their parent's behavior. It is for this reason that as we grow up we find in ourselves some familiar personality traits. Impatience is no exception.

A person who has an impatient nature is often one who has learned to be like that within their family context. We do not want to point "culprits" for our impatient behavior, but education is important as an element that interferes with our reactions, both in childhood and in adulthood.

The most important thing is to ask yourself about it. If your parents were impatient during your childhood, chances are you are impatient now. However, you can change and adapt your mind by using strategies to be a better person. Train your resilience, benevolence, love, understanding, compassion, forgiveness, gratitude, tolerance… and patience!

**"If you cannot do everything,
do everything you can."**

No one says that patience is easy. Everyone has moments when we want to throw it all away—and that is normal.

Like any behavioral competence, serenity needs to be trained.

Therefore, it is essential to find ways to recharge your patience and regain your pace.

# | AVOIDING ALIOTH |

# | EXERCISES TO AVOID ALIOTH |



During various situations of chaos and impatience, remember to avoid **ALIOTH**. Ty to observe yourself and then perform the exercises using the **"4S"** rule.

**Key Signs of Impatience**

Always in a hurry

Legs and feet shaking

Irritability

Outbursts

Tense muscles

Hard breathing

# Always in a hurry

Meditate that time will be enough for you to solve everything you want. If it is not, more time will come and you can use it to complement your tasks. Be positive, use the "yes" to convince yourself that you do not have to hurry so much. Try to calm down, and believe that this agitation to comply with a schedule, so full of activities, is not worth it. Decrease your number of daily tasks. Reformulate your schedule. Talk to people who can help you, both at work and at home. Share your tasks. Remember that no one is irreplaceable.

# Legs and feet shaking

Observe your body. Are your feet restless? Do your legs keep moving? How about taking a few minutes to bring the calmness to you? Sit comfortably somewhere, or even remain where you are, but close your eyes. Breathe and focus on your heart, soothing every part of your body. *Smile* to life. Smile to yourself. Be grateful for the possibility of mastering your anxiety. Cultivate positive, quiet emotion. This is not lost time—it is revealing moments that will bring you health and peace.

# Irritability

Listen to what you say. Look at your own tense features and your own frowning face. Realize how unpleasant you are being to others, to the situation, and to yourself. *Silence.* Try to stop talking, complaining, and misusing your time of existence. Believe that you can love the world more if you are more benevolent to those who bother you or more resilient in the face of the difficult situations you are facing. *Yes.* You are capable of overcoming adversity, suffering, and pressure.

# Outbursts

Stop being rude. Spend a few moments in *silence*. Stay away from people who are annoying you and listen to nature, such as the song of the birds, the wind that blows in the trees, or a dog that barks in the distance. Your mind begins to shut down, reaching for different vibrations. Forget the anger that dominates you and *smile* at the nature that surrounds you. How many people would like to hear these sounds or see the scenarios you are admiring? Be thankful by replacing your mood outbursts with positive head movements: *yes*. Agree that you are privileged to have so many possibilities for change and friends who support you, and bring back patience to yourself. *Sigh* and continue your learning journey. This journey is merely beginning. It will be difficult, but quite pleasurable.

# Tense muscles

Move your head sideways. The noise is your vertebrae popping and showing the stiffness of your neck. Notice how your shoulders are raised, signaling an alert posture. Does your body hurt? Notice how tense your muscles are. Give a deep *sigh*, releasing the air while mentalizing that you are releasing the negative energies that pressure you. Again, inhale hard and exhale mentalizing that your body is throwing out everything that distresses you. *Smile*, because you are beginning to reflect on what bothers you and to discover ways to sow calmness within you.

# Hard breathing

Breathe to calm your stress and restore yourself in seconds. The *sigh*, the deep and slow breathing through the nose, is exactly what you need when impatience is threatening to arrive. When we are impatient, the shortness of breath is usually an accelerated breathing that only hinders our harmony. Emotional factors and desperate reactions to the pressures of life also cause a shortness of breath. Faced with a stressful situation, also called a "stressor," the heart races and breathing becomes short, and we have difficulty controlling the entry and exit of air. A rapid respiratory movement makes breathing shallow and lung air is not renewed efficiently. As a result, we lack oxygen and we suffocate and panic, which leads to unwanted impatience. Pay attention to your breathing when you are like this. You can also have a moment of apnea, with the breath withheld, and want to release that breath by screaming or talking loudly in a form of explosion from the loss of patience.

Try the relaxation and breathing exercises to regain your composure and regain your breath. Nasal breathing helps to soothe these anxiety attacks and restore your calm. Inhale calmly through your nose, inflating your chest like a balloon. Then hold your breath for a few seconds. Exhale deeply through your nose, compressing your stomach and abdomen, until all the air comes out.

# | CONCLUSION:
## 10 LESSONS ON PATIENCE |

**1** Daily exercises will appear in each person's daily life according to their lifestyle. The cultivation of patience makes you more tolerant and improves your coexistence with everyone and everything. You tolerate provocations without reacting, and you also face illness, pain, and suffering more calmly. You become a more pleasant companion for other people, who feel treated better, whether at home or at work. Most people need to practice patience a significant amount to truly make it a habit. Do not expect to be more patient overnight, as it takes significant effort and practice. You need to exercise.

**2** The cultivation of full patience involves the control of stress, anger, fear, anxiety, worries, and the practice of experiences that embody peace and well-being. To improve your full patience you must develop inner tranquility, calmness and serenity, and emotions opposed to irritation, restlessness and anger, which are siblings of impatience. The mind, in a receptive state, a state of rest, is calm, serene, and full of peace; therefore, to expand your patience, you must integrate it into your life in a full and conscious way, remembering that patience only works if it is complete.

**3** For you to cultivate patience, you should practice the following steps: first, make the decision to be patient with yourself and others by making a "written and signed commitment" to yourself. Then, practice the "4S" method. When you feel your mind agitated, take a deep breath and say to yourself, "4S," and repeatedly remember the sequence learned here, until you get better: silence, smile, sigh, and sure.

**4** Controlling your stress and negative emotions and replacing them with positive ones is critical. You should also be tolerant and understanding of yourself. Moreover, remember that people are not obliged to fulfill your desires, and they must be respected.

**5** Cultivate patience by walking slowly and doing your chores without hurry. Time is your friend, for it is the present.

**6** Practice mindfulness and continuously watch your mind to identify impatient thoughts. In other words, identify the "enemies of patience," perhaps even the three at the same time. Be alert, but do it calmly as you know what they are and you know how to deal with them.

**7** To incorporate an experience of feeling peace and well-being, first relax. Then pay attention to your body and see if anything bothers you. Next, look around and see if there is anything "threatening." Remove any fear from the mind, along with worry, anxiety, irritation, or anger. Be quiet.

**8** Thank those who are the source of your impatience. They are actually giving you free exercises to train your full patience. By considering the people who disturb you with gratitude, you will react differently, seeing their actions as an "exercise to be faced," and as a possibility to continue to practice full patience.

**9** Keep the feeling of relaxation in your memory and let it penetrate for a few minutes into your mind and body. Extend this sensation as much as you can by activating the "4S" rule, and temporarily forget about your problems. In the first hour after training, only think of neutral or positive thoughts.

**10** If you have a special talent to develop but lack patience, you will never be able to turn it into an accomplishment. Try to focus your attention and desire on your dreams patiently. Although many people you admire may be naturally creative, innovative, and intelligent, they got where they are thanks to dedication and patience.

*"Our patience will always accomplish more than all our strengths."*

# | EPILOGUE—COSTA G. |

When I received the invitation from my son, Pedro Costa, to participate in this project, I took a few minutes to answer. The theme was intriguing, the partner was a special person, and I really love writing. Why not?

At the time, he had already formatted an idea about the basis of the text: a path that would help people achieve full patience. Pedro was already writing about this idea of his. I thought it best to read "diagonally," without dwelling too much on the details of the text and to start my work. Taking a certain distance was necessary so that I could find my way on the subject.

Then came the idea of me also doing the illustrations. As a visual artist, I work with characters from popular culture. As a teacher of graphic design, I followed many discussions and teachings on illustrative productions, but I never executed any. It would be yet another challenge. Instead, I accepted! I decided to start from a "being," somewhat hybrid, with a simple and striking shape, that could, through facial expressions, portray their feelings and emotions throughout the passages of the book. It is a character immersed in the problems of patience and impatience that surround daily life, like each one of us.

Working on this project was quite a partnership. After I prepared each text, I sent it so Pedro to adapt it to the base text. With each writing I learned more and more about my own difficulties in relation to the theme, which helped me to manage the reflections and conclusions on this vast and difficult subject. We read the text several times, weaving corrections and adjustments and formatting the construction so that it became a single work, made by two hands.

I am not a patient person, though some might think it. I am also not a chronically "impatient" person. I think I have my moments of serenity and also of restlessness, like any human being. Spirituality and the practice of yoga and meditation were fundamental for me to survive some difficult confrontations. I am constantly learning, and this is how I wish to shape my journey through this existence.

The paths traced in this book were effectively tested by both of us. I remember several conversations in which we confessed our personal experiences with the "friends of patience": "today I am testing the sure," "really, the silence helps so much." We also confided in each other about some daily confrontations that we were going through with family and friends in different situations, and using, in practice, the content of the writings.

It was a wonderful experience, as a proud mother, as a writer in training, as a beginner illustrator, and, above all, as an apprentice of life, treading roads of learning! I hope the reading was as pleasurable and helpful to you as it was to me.

I am very grateful for your patience.

# FULL PATIENCE

**People** take your calm
The **lack of time** is a torment
Apply the four friends
That will bring you respite

The friends of patience
**SMILE**, **SIGH,** and **SURE**
They form the quartet of **S**
Together with **SILENCE** at last

Bringing people together
The **SMILE** is always a weapon
Blossoming patience
Illuminating the soul

**Too many things** to do
There is an anti-stress solution
**SIGH** and move on
Learn from another **S**

**On the road of life**
Do not always respond with action
Simple, hold your words
**SILENCE** is the solution

**SURE** also starts with **S**
He is a great advisor
Opens doors and paths
No doubt, another partner

Live quietly and smilingly
Apply **full patience**
Live in the present time
Today and always like a poem

# | EPILOGUE – COSTA P. |

How can I explain my entry into this area and even the writing of a book on such a particular subject as full patience? Simply because I am an impatient person. Patience, in the field of medicine, is a vital quality in the workplace, and I needed to cultivate it to get where I am. It reduces stress and conflict, leads to better relationships, and helps achieve short- and long-term life and career goals.

I have often struggled with impatience. I learned to recognize the physical and emotional symptoms associated with it and identified the situations that trigger it. When I understood the causes of my impatience, I began to develop strategies to prevent or overcome it. The "4S" technique was a way to remind me how to act and what to do to feel better. With this, I was able to take care of my physical well-being using deep breathing and relaxation techniques, in addition to developing my empathy and emotional intelligence skills. Over the years, I have learned that all we feel are emotions. It is also our emotions that drive us to do important things, such as confessing our feelings for a loved one. Writing this book with my beloved mother was an indescribable experience. The understanding of emotions, therefore, plays a primary role in our life.

What can we do to have more pleasant feelings and maintain a better relationship with others and with our self? We have to get to know our emotions! Unfortunately, we do not always have "time" to decode the messages of our body and soul. We fall into "situations" that we do not want, or "people" are placed in our lives without us asking them to be part of it. It is life... and we need to learn from it. When we experience an emotion like "impatience," our brain partially loses its ability to control: I did not want to feel this way. What led me to wish to write this book was the desire to improve as a human being, as a father, as a professional, as a partner, and to share something that impatient people could put into practice, since we are all a little bit like that. My home, my work, and the streets became like a "laboratory" for my learning. The fact of having two children at home during the writing of the book and being aware that I did not react the way I wanted due to a lack of "tools" made me reflect on what it meant for my children, for example, to have a patient and calm person helping their well-being. Silence was fundamental, breathing was constantly present, the smile changed every moment, and the yes affirmed that I had control of myself. I began to experience the method and reflect on it, I shared it with my mother, the co-author of this book, and we passed on our learning to our readers.

# | SPECIAL THANKS |

As a mother and son writing together in a pleasant way, we can begin by stating that we are grateful to life, which gave us this parental relationship nourished by love and trust that continues to draw paths of coexistence, harmony, and learning. We are mutually grateful for the partnership in the writing of this book, as well as for the exchanges, opinions, tolerance, the exercise of benevolence, trust, and especially patience, which underpinned our work together. To produce a work with four hands, this experience was a lesson about how to conjugate essential verbs: maintain, exchange, accept, yield, listen, learn, withdraw, and correct. All without impositions or selfishness.

We thank everyone who, in one way or another and even without having been aware of it, participated in the execution of this book. Thank you to the friends and relatives who live with us and are so precious that they make us want to change and improve as individuals, for their sake. We would also like to thank acquaintances and strangers who make us lose our patience daily or sporadically. Without them, there would be no "human laboratory," which is essential to reflect on our attitudes towards patience and the lack of it.

A thank you also goes to Hugo Henrique de Araújo Azevedo, who helped us in the textual revision, always bringing such precise and enlightening guidelines. We also thank future graphic designer, Mateus Rocha de Carvalho, for formatting the design and cover.

We would like to give a special thanks to Nun Coen for accepting our invitation to write the preface to the book. Her positive response was a pleasant surprise and a real proof of her humility and dedication. We are honored by such a significant participation, bringing us the teachings of Buddhism and her own perspective, which emphasize the importance of full patience for the formation of the being and consequently of all humanity.

And last, we thank you, readers, who have patiently come this far.

# |ÍNDICE|